THE WOODSON SERIES

A CENTURY OF NEGRO MIGRATION

Carter Godwin Woodson

THE WOODSON SERIES

A CENTURY OF NEGRO MIGRATION

Carter Godwin Woodson

Black Classic Press
Baltimore

A Century of Negro Migration

Published 2019 by Black Classic Press

Library of Congress Control Number: 2019932262

Print book ISBN: 978-1-57478-166-3
E-book ISBN: 978-1-57478-167-0

Cover design by Mitchell & Sennaar Communications, Inc.

Printed by BCP Digital Printing (www.bcpdigital.com)
an affiliate company of Black Classic Press Inc.
For a virtual tour of our publishing and printing facility visit:
https://www.c-span.org/video/?441322-2/tour-black-classic-press

Purchase Black Classic Press books from your favorite book seller
or online at: www.blackclassicbooks.com

For inquiries or to request a list of titles, write:
Black Classic Press
P.O. Box 13414
Baltimore, MD 21203

Introduction to the Woodson Series

The Association for the Study of African American Life and History (ASALH) is pleased to partner with Black Classic Press to make available the works published by the Associated Publishers (AP.) Founded by Carter G. Woodson in 1921, the Associated Publishers dedicated itself to bringing to the public works by and about Africans and people of African descent that could not find a home among mainstream publishers.

For decades, Black Classic Press has distinguished itself as a company dedicated to ensuring that important works remain before the reading public. Moreover, the proprietor, Paul Coates, has been a stalwart supporter of ASALH and an exemplar of Woodson's philosophy that important knowledge about Black people must be available.

When Carter G. Woodson passed away on April 3, 1950, the Association he founded became the majority stockholder of the publishing house and continued to carry the mission forward. Over the years, the press was run by the giants of the Association, including Benjamin Quarles and Edgar Toppin. Yet, Miss W. Leona Miles was the day-to-day presence. She labored alongside of Carter G. Woodson during his last years, and continued to manage the AP until her own death in the 1990s. By the late 1990s, the publishing agenda of the Association had waned and, in 2005, the corporation was dissolved. Since then, ASALH has published directly through its own imprint, the ASALH Press.

The partnership between ASALH and the Black Classic Press could not have come at a better time: the centennial of the founding of Woodson's Association in 1915. The works will appear as originally published in their final editions. The Woodson Series will not only bring "Black Classics" back to life but do so at the major milestone in the history of the study of Black life, history, and culture.

Daryl Michael Scott, President of ASALH, 2013-2014

To my Father
JAMES WOODSON
WHO MADE IT POSSIBLE FOR ME
TO ENTER THE LITERARY WORLD

PREFACE

IN treating this movement of the Negroes, the writer does not presume to say the last word on the subject. The exodus of the Negroes from the South has just begun. The blacks have recently realized that they have freedom of body and they will now proceed to exercise that right. To presume, therefore, to exhaust the treatment of this movement in its incipiency is far from the intention of the writer. The aim here is rather to direct attention to this new phase of Negro American life which will doubtless prove to be the most significant event in our local history since the Civil War.

Many of the facts herein set forth have seen light before. The effort here is directed toward an original treatment of facts, many of which have already periodically appeared in some form. As these works, however, are too numerous to be consulted by the layman, the writer has endeavored to present in succinct form the leading facts as to how the Negroes in the United States have struggled under adverse circumstances to flee from bondage and oppression in quest of a land offering asylum to the oppressed and opportunity to the unfortunate. How they have often been deceived has been carefully noted.

Preface

With the hope that this volume may interest another worker to the extent of publishing many other facts in this field, it is respectfully submitted to the public.

CARTER G. WOODSON.

WASHINGTON, D. C.,
March 31, 1918.

CONTENTS

MAPS AND DIAGRAMS

CHAPTER I

THE migration of the blacks from the Southern States to those offering them better opportunities is nothing new. The objective here, therefore, will be not merely to present the causes and results of the recent movement of the Negroes to the North but to connect this event with the periodical movements of the blacks to that section, from about the year 1815 to the present day. That this movement should date from that period indicates that the policy of the commonwealths towards the Negro must have then begun decidedly to differ so as to make one section of the country more congenial to the despised blacks than the other. As a matter of fact, to justify this conclusion, we need but give passing mention here to developments too well known to be discussed in detail. Slavery in the original thirteen States was the normal condition of the Negroes. When, however, James Otis, Patrick Henry and Thomas Jefferson began to discuss the natural rights of the colonists, then said to be oppressed by Great Britain, some of the patriots of the Revolution carried their reasoning to its logical conclusion, contending that the Negro slaves should be

1

freed on the same grounds, as their rights were also founded in the laws of nature.[1] And so it was soon done in most Northern commonwealths. Vermont, New Hampshire, and Massachusetts exterminated the institution by constitutional provision and Rhode Island, Connecticut, New Jersey, New York and Pennsylvania by gradual emancipation acts.[2] And it was thought that the institution would soon thereafter pass away even in all southern commonwealths except South Carolina and Georgia, where it had seemingly become profitable. There came later the industrial revolution following the invention of Watt's steam engine and mechanical appliances like Whitney's cotton gin, all which changed the economic aspect of the modern world, making slavery an institution offering means of exploitation to those engaged in the production of cotton. This revolution rendered necessary a large supply of cheap labor for cotton culture, out of which the plantation system grew. The Negro slaves, therefore, lost all hope of ever winning their freedom in South Carolina and Georgia; and in Maryland, Virginia, and North Carolina, where the sentiment in favor of abolition had been favorable, there was

---

[1] Locke, *Anti-Slavery*, pp. 19, 20, 23; *Works of John Woolman*, pp. 58, 73; and Moore, *Notes on Slavery in Massachusetts*, p. 71.

[2] Bassett, *Federalist System*, chap. xii. Hart, *Slavery and Abolition*, pp. 153, 154.

a decided reaction which soon blighted their hopes.[3] In the Northern commonwealths, however, the sentiment in behalf of universal freedom, though at times dormant, was ever apparent despite the attachment to the South of the trading classes of northern cities, which profited by the slave trade and their commerce with the slaveholding States. The Northern States maintaining this liberal attitude developed, therefore, into an asylum for the Negroes who were oppressed in the South.

The Negroes, however, were not generally welcomed in the North. Many of the northerners who sympathized with the oppressed blacks in the South never dreamt of having them as their neighbors. There were, consequently, always two classes of anti-slavery people, those who advocated the abolition of slavery to elevate the blacks to the dignity of citizenship, and those who merely hoped to exterminate the institution because it was an economic evil.[4] The latter generally believed that the blacks constituted an inferior class that could not discharge the duties of citizenship, and when the proposal to incorporate the blacks into the body politic was clearly presented to these agitators their anti-slavery ardor was decidedly dampened. Unwilling, however, to take the position that a

[3] Turner, *The Rise of the New West*, pp. 45, 46, 47, 48, 49; Hammond, *Cotton Industry*, chaps. i and ii; Scherer, *Cotton as a World Power*, pp. 168, 175.

[4] Locke, *Anti-Slavery*, chaps. i and ii.

race should be doomed because of personal objections, many of the early anti-slavery group looked toward colonization for a solution of this problem.[5] Some thought of Africa, but since the deportation of a large number of persons who had been brought under the influence of modern civilization seemed cruel, the most popular colonization scheme at first seemed to be that of settling the Negroes on the public lands in the West. As this region had been lately ceded, however, and no one could determine what use could be made of it by white men, no such policy was generally accepted.

When this territory was ceded to the United States an effort to provide for the government of it finally culminated in the proposed Ordinance of 1784 carrying the provision that slavery should not exist in the Northwest Territory after the year 1800.[6] This measure finally failed to pass and fortunately too, thought some, because, had slavery been given sixteen years of growth on that soil, it might not have been abolished there until the Civil War or it might have caused such a preponderance of slave commonwealths as to make the rebellion successful. The Ordinance of 1784 was antecedent to the more important Ordinance of 1787, which carried the famous sixth article that neither slavery nor involuntary servitude except as a

[5] Jay, *An Inquiry*, p. 30.

[6] Ford edition, *Jefferson's Writings*, III, p. 432.

punishment for crime should exist in that territory. At first, it was generally deemed feasible to establish Negro colonies on that domain. Yet despite the assurance of the Ordinance of 1787 conditions were such that one could not determine exactly whether the Northwest Territory would be slave or free.[7]

What then was the situation in this partly unoccupied territory? Slavery existed in what is now the Northwest Territory from the time of the early exploration and settlement of that region by the French. The first slaves of white men were Indians. Though it is true that the red men usually chose death rather than slavery, there were some of them that bowed to the yoke. So many Pawnee Indians became bondsmen that the word *Pani* became synonymous with slave in the West.[8] Western Indians themselves, following the custom of white men, enslaved their captives in war rather than choose the alternative of putting them to death. In this way they were known to hold a number of blacks and whites.

[7] For the passage of this ordinance three reasons have been given: Slavery then prior to the invention of the cotton gin was considered a necessary evil in the South. The expected monopoly of the tobacco and indigo cultivation in the South would be promoted by excluding Negroes from the Northwest Territory and thus preventing its cultivation there. Dr. Cutler's influence aided by Mr. Grayson of Virginia was of much assistance. The philanthropic idea was not so prominent as men have thought.—Dunn, *Indiana*, p. 212.

[8] *Ibid.*, p. 254.

The enslavement of the black man by the whites in this section dates from the early part of the eighteenth century. Being a part of the Louisiana Territory which under France extended over the whole Mississippi Valley as far as the Allegheny mountains, it was governed by the same colonial regulations.[9] Slavery, therefore, had legal standing in this territory. When Antoine Crozat, upon being placed in control of Louisiana, was authorized to begin a traffic in slaves, Crozat himself did nothing to carry out his plan. But in 1717 when the control of the colony was transferred to the *Compagnie de l'Occident* steps were taken toward the importation of slaves. In 1719, when 500 Guinea Negroes were brought over to serve in Lower Louisiana, Philip Francis Renault imported 500 other bondsmen into Upper Louisiana or what was later included in the Northwest Territory. Slavery then became more and more extensive until by 1750 there were along the Mississippi five settlements of slaves, Kaskaskia, Kaokia, Fort Chartres, St. Phillipe and Prairie du Rocher.[10] In 1763 Negroes were relatively

[9] *Code Noir.*

[10] Speaking of these settlements in 1750, M. Viner, a Jesuit Missionary to the Indians, said: ''We have here Whites, Negroes, and Indians, to say nothing of cross-breeds—There are five French villages and three villages of the natives within a space of twenty-one leagues—In the five French villages there are perhaps eleven hundred whites, three hundred blacks, and some sixty red slaves or savages.''

numerous in the Northwest Territory but when this section that year was transferred to the British the number was diminished by the action of those Frenchmen who, unwilling to become subjects of Great Britain, moved from the territory.[11] There was no material increase in the slave population thereafter until the end of the

Unlike the condition of the slaves in Lower Louisiana where the rigid enforcement of the Slave Code made their lives almost intolerable, the slaves of the Northwest Territory were for many reasons much more fortunate. In the first place, subject to the control of a mayor-commandant appointed by the Governor of New Orleans, the early dwellers in this territory managed their plantations about as they pleased. Moreover, as there were few planters who owned as many as three or four Negroes, slavery in the Northwest Territory did not get far beyond the patriarchal stage. Slaves were usually well fed. The relations between master and slave were friendly. The bondsmen were allowed special privileges on Sundays and holidays and their children were taught the catechism according to the ordinance of Louis XIV in 1724, which provided that all masters should educate their slaves in the Apostolic Catholic religion and have them baptized. Male slaves were worked side by side in the fields with their masters and the female slaves in neat attire went with their mistresses to matins and vespers. Slaves freely mingled in practically all festive enjoyments.—See *Jesuit Relations*, LXIX, p. 144; Hutchins, *An Historical Narrative*, 1784; and *Code Noir*.

11 Mention was thereafter made of slaves as in the case of Captain Philip Pittman who in 1770 wrote of one Mr. Beauvais, ''who owned 240 orpens of cultivated land and eighty slaves; and such a case as that of a Captain of a militia at St. Philips, possessing twenty blacks; and the case of Mr. Bales, a very rich man of St. Genevieve, Illinois, owning a hundred Negroes, beside having white people constantly employed.''—See Captain Pittman's *The Present State of the European Settlements in the Mississippi*, 1770.

eighteenth century when some Negroes came from the original thirteen.

The Ordinance of 1787 did not disturb the relation of slave and master. Some pioneers thought that the sixth article exterminated slavery there; others contended that it did not. The latter believed that such expressions in the Ordinance of 1787 as the ''free inhabitants'' and the ''free male inhabitants of full size'' implied the continuance of slavery and others found ground for its perpetuation in that clause of the Ordinance which allowed the people of the territory to adopt the constitution and laws of any one of the thirteen States. Students of law saw protection for slavery in Jay's treaty which guaranteed to the settlers their property of all kinds.[12] When, therefore, the slave question came up in the Northwest Territory about the close of the eighteenth century, there were three classes of slaves: first, those who were in servitude to French owners previous to the cession of the Territory to England and were still claimed as property in the possession of which the owners were protected under the treaty of 1763; second, those who were held by British owners at the time of Jay's treaty and claimed afterward as property under its protection; and third, those who, since the Territory had been controlled by the United States, had been brought from the commonwealths in which slav-

12 Dunn, *Indiana*, chap. vi.

ery was allowed.[13] Freedom, however, was recognized as the ultimate status of the Negro in that territory.

This question having been seemingly settled, Anthony Benezet, who for years advocated the abolition of slavery and devoted his time and means to the preparation of the Negroes for living as freedmen, was practical enough to recommend to the Congress of the Confederation a plan of colonizing the emancipated blacks on the western lands.[14] Jefferson incorporated into his scheme for a modern system of public schools the training of the slaves in industrial and agricultural branches to equip them for a higher station in life. He believed, however, that the blacks not being equal to the white race should not be assimilated and should they be free, they should, by all means, be colonized afar off.[15] Thinking that the western lands might be so used, he said in writing to James Monroe in 1801: "A very great extent of country north of the Ohio has been laid off in townships, and is now at market, according to the provisions of the act of Congress. . . . There is nothing," said he, "which would restrain the State of Virginia either in the purchase or the

13 Hinsdale, *Old Northwest*, p. 350.
14 *Tyrannical Libertymen*, pp. 10, 11; Locke, *Anti-Slavery*, pp. 31, 32; Brannagan, *Serious Remonstrance*, p. 18.
15 Washington edition of *Jefferson's Writings*, chap. vi, p. 456, and chap. viii, p. 380.

application of these lands.''[16]   Yet he raised the
question as to whether the establishment of such
a colony within our limits and to become a part
of the Union would be desirable. He thought
then of procuring a place beyond the limits of
the United States on our northern boundary,
by purchasing the Indian lands with the consent
of Great Britain. He then doubted that the black
race would live in such a rigorous climate.

This plan did not easily pass from the minds
of the friends of the slaves, for in 1805 Thomas
Brannagan asserted in his *Serious Remonstrances* that the government should appro-
priate a few thousand acres of land at some dis-
tant part of the national domains for the Negroes' accommodation and support. He believed that the new State might be established
upwards of 2,000 miles from our frontier.[17]   A
copy of the pamphlet containing this proposi-
tion was sent to Thomas Jefferson, who was impressed thereby, but not having the courage to
brave the torture of being branded as a friend
of the slave, he failed to give it his support.[18]
The same question was brought prominently before the public again in 1816 when there was
presented to the House of Representatives a
memorial from the Kentucky Abolition Society
praying that the free people of color be colonized

16 Ford edition of *Jefferson's Writings*, III, pp. 244; IX, p.
303; X, pp. 76, 290.

17 Brannagan, *Serious Remonstrances*, p. 18.

18 Library edition of *Jefferson's Writings*, X, pp. 295, 296.

on the public lands. The committee to whom
the memorial was referred for consideration
reported that it was expedient to refuse the request on the ground that, as such lands were not
granted to free white men, they saw no reason
for granting them to others.[19]

Some Negro slaves unwilling to wait to be
carried or invited to the Northwest Territory
escaped to that section even when it was controlled by the French prior to the American
Revolution. Slaves who reached the West by
this route caused trouble between the French
and the British colonists. Advertising in 1746
for James Wenyam, a slave, Richard Colgate,
his master, said that he swore to a Negro whom
he endeavored to induce to go with him, that he
had often been in the backwoods with his master and that he would go to the French and Indians and fight for them.[20] In an advertise-
ment for a mulatto slave in 1755 Thomas Rin-
gold, his master, expressed fear that he had escaped by the same route to the French. He,
therefore, said: "It seems to be the interest, at
least, of every gentleman that has slaves, to be
active in the beginning of these attempts, for
whilst we have the French such near neighbors,
we shall not have the least security in that kind
of property."[21]

[19] Adams, *Neglected Period of Anti-Slavery*, pp. 129, 130.
[20] *The Pennsylvania Gazette*, July 31, 1746.
[21] *The Maryland Gazette*, March 20, 1755.

The good treatment which these slaves received among the French, and especially at Pittsburgh the gateway to the Northwest Territory, tended to make that city an asylum for those slaves who had sufficient spirit of adventure to brave the wilderness through which they had to go. Negroes even then had the idea that there was in this country a place of more privilege than those they enjoyed in the seaboard colonies. Knowing of the likelihood of the Negroes to rise during the French and Indian War, Governor Dinwiddie wrote Fox one of the Secretaries of State in 1756: "We dare not venture to part with any of our white men any distance, as we must have a watchful eye over our Negro slaves, who are upward of one hundred thousand."[22] Brissot de Warville mentions in his *Travels of 1788* several examples of marriages of white and blacks in Pittsburgh. He noted the case of a Negro who married an indentured French servant woman. Out of this union came a desirable mulatto girl who married a surgeon of Nantes then stationed at Pittsburgh. His family was considered one of the most respectable of the city. The Negro referred to was doing a creditable business and his wife took it upon herself to welcome foreigners, especially the French, who came that way. Along the Ohio also there were several cases of women of color living with unmarried

[22] *Washington's Writings*, II, p. 134.

white men; but this was looked upon by the Negroes as detestable as was evidenced by the fact that, if black women had a quarrel with a mulatto woman, the former would reproach the latter for being of ignoble blood.[23] These tendencies, however, could not assure the Negro that the Northwest Territory was to be an asylum for freedom when in 1763 it passed into the hands of the British, the promoters of the slave trade, and later to the independent colonies, two of which had no desire to exterminate slavery. Furthermore, when the Ordinance of 1787 with its famous sixth article against slavery was proclaimed, it was soon discovered that this document was not necessarily emancipatory. As the right to hold slaves was guaranteed to those who owned them prior to the passage of the Ordinance of 1787, it was to be expected that those attached to that institution would not indifferently see it pass away. Various petitions, therefore, were sent to the territorial legislature and to Congress praying that the sixth article of the Ordinance of 1787 be abrogated.[24] No formal action to this effect was taken, but the practice of slavery was continued even at the winking of the government. Some slaves came from the Canadians who, in accordance with the slave trade laws of the British

[23] Brissot de Warville, *New Travels*, II, pp. 33–34.

[24] Harris, *Slavery in Illinois*, chaps. iii, iv, and v; Dunn, *Indiana*, pp. 218–260; Hinsdale, *Old Northwest*, pp. 351–358.

Empire, were supplied with bondsmen. It was the Canadians themselves who provided by act of parliament in 1793 for prohibiting the importation of slaves and for gradual emancipation. When it seemed later that the cause of freedom would eventually triumph the proslavery element undertook to perpetuate slavery through a system of indentured servant labor. In the formation of the States of Indiana and Illinois the question as to what should be done to harmonize with the new constitution the system of indenture to which the territorial legislatures had been committed, caused heated debate and at times almost conflict. Both Indiana[25] and Illinois[26] finally incorporated into

25 This code provided that all male Negroes under fifteen years of age either owned or acquired must remain in servitude until they reached the age of thirty-five and female slaves until thirty-two. The male children of such persons held to service could be bound out for thirty years and the female children for twenty-eight. Slaves brought into the territory had to comply with contracts for terms of service when their master registered them within thirty days from the time he brought them into the territory. Indentured black servants were not exactly sold, but the law permitted the transfer from one owner to another when the slave acquiesced in the transfer before a notary, but it was often done without regard to the slave. They were even bequeathed and sold as personal property at auction. Notices for sale were frequent. There were rewards for runaway slaves. Negroes whose terms had almost expired were kidnapped and sold to New Orleans. The legislature imposed a penalty for such, but it was not generally enforced. They were taxable property valued according to the length of service. Negroes served as laborers on farms, house servants, and in salt mines, the latter being an excuse for holding them as

their constitutions compromise provisions for a nominal prohibition of slavery modified by clauses for the continuation of the system of indentured labor of the Negroes held to service. The proslavery party persistently struggled for some years to secure by the interpretation of the laws, by legislation and even by amending the constitution so to change the fundamental law as to provide for actual slavery. These States,however, gradually worked toward freedom in keeping with the spirit of the majority who framed the constitution, despite the

slaves. Persons of color could purchase servants of their own race. The law provided that the Justice of the County could on complaint from the master order that a lazy servant be whipped. In this frontier section, therefore, where men often took the law in their own hands, slaves were often punished and abused just as they were in the Southern States. The law dealing with fugitives was somewhat harsh. When apprehended, fugitives had to serve two days extra for each day they lost from their master's service. The harboring of a runaway slave was punishable by a fine of one day for each the slave might be concealed. Consistently too with the provision of the laws in most slave States, slaves could retain all goods or money lawfully acquired during their servitude provided their master gave his consent. Upon the demonstration of proof to the county court that they had served their term they could obtain from that tribunal certificates of freedom. See *The Laws of Indiana.*

26 Masters had to provide adequate food, and clothing and good lodging for the slave, but the penalty for failing to comply with this law was not clear and even if so, it happened that many masters never observed it. There was also an effort to prevent cruelty to slaves, but it was difficult to establish the guilt of masters when the slave could not bear witness against his owner and it was not likely that the neighbor equally guilty

fact that the indenture system in southern Illinois and especially in Indiana was at times tantamount to slavery as it was practiced in parts of the South.

It must be borne in mind here, however, that the North at this time was far from becoming a place of refuge for Negroes. In the first place, the industrial revolution had not then had time to reduce the Negroes to the plane of beasts in the cotton kingdom. The rigorous climate and the industries of the northern people, moreover, were not inviting to the blacks and the development of the carrying trade and the rise of manufacturing there did not make that section

or indifferent to the complaints of the blacks would take their petitions to court.

Under this system a large number of slaves were brought into the Territory especially after 1807. There were 135 in 1800. This increase came from Kentucky and Tennessee. As those brought were largely boys and girls with a long period of service, this form of slavery was assured for some years. The children of these blacks were often registered for thirty-five instead of thirty years of service on the ground that they were not born in Illinois. No one thought of persecuting a master for holding servants unlawfully and Negroes themselves could be easily deceived. Very few settlers brought their slaves there to free them. There were only 749 in 1820. If one considers the proportion of this to the number brought there for manumission this seems hardly true. It is better to say that during these first two decades of the nineteenth century some settlers came for both purposes, some to hold slaves, some, as Edward Coles, to free them. It was not only practiced in the southern part along the Mississippi and Ohio but as far north in Illinois as Sangamon County, were found servants known as "yellow boys" and "colored girls."—See the *Laws of Illinois*.

more attractive to unskilled labor. Furthermore, when we consider the fact that there were
many thousands of Negroes in the Southern
States the presence of a few in the North must
be regarded as insignificant. This paucity of
blacks then obtained especially in the Northwest Territory, for its French inhabitants instead of being an exploiting people were pioneering, having little use for slaves in carrying out
their policy of merely holding the country for
France. Moreover, like certain gentlemen from
Virginia, who after the American Revolution
were afraid to bring their slaves with them to
occupy their bounty lands in Ohio, few enterprising settlers from the slave States had invaded the territory with their Negroes, not
knowing whether or not they would be secure
in the possession of such property. When we
consider that in 1810 there were only 102,137
Negroes in the North and no more than 3,454 in
the Northwest Territory, we must look to the
second decade of the nineteenth century for the
beginning of the migration of the Negroes in
the United States.

CHAPTER II

A TRANSPLANTATION TO THE NORTH

JUST after the settlement of the question of holding the western posts by the British and the adjustment of the trouble arising from their capture of slaves during our second war with England, there started a movement of the blacks to this frontier territory. But, as there were few towns or cities in the Northwest during the first decades of the new republic, the flight of the Negro into that territory was like that of a fugitive taking his chances in the wilderness. Having lost their pioneering spirit in passing through the ordeal of slavery, not many of the bondmen took flight in that direction and few free Negroes ventured to seek their fortunes in those wilds during the period of the frontier conditions, especially when the country had not then undergone a thorough reaction against the Negro.

The migration of the Negroes, however, received an impetus early in the nineteenth century. This came from the Quakers, who by the middle of the eighteenth century had taken the position that all members of their sect should free their slaves.[1] The Quakers of North Caro-

[1] Moore, *Anti-Slavery*, p. 79; and *Special Report of the United States Commissioner of Education*, 1871, p. 376; Weeks, *Southern Quakers*, pp. 215, 216, 231, 232, 242.

lina and Virginia had as early as 1740 taken up the serious question of humanely treating their Negroes. The North Carolina Quakers advised Friends to emancipate their slaves, later prohibited traffic in them, forbade their members from even hiring the blacks out in 1780 and by 1818 had exterminated the institution among their communicants.[2] After healing themselves of the sin, they had before the close of the eighteenth century militantly addressed themselves to the task of abolishing slavery and the slave trade throughout the world. Differing in their scheme from that of most anti-slavery leaders, they were advocating the establishment of the freedmen in society as good citizens and to that end had provided for the religious and mental instruction of their slaves prior to emancipating them.[3]

Despite the fact that the Quakers were not free to extend their operations throughout the colonies, they did much to enable the Negroes to reach free soil. As the Quakers believed in the freedom of the will, human brotherhood, and equality before God, they did not, like the Puritans, find difficulties in solving the problem of elevating the Negroes. Whereas certain Puritans were afraid that conversion might lead to the destruction of caste and the incorporation

[2] *The Southern Workman*, xxvii, p. 161.

[3] Rhodes, *History of the United States*, chap. i, p. 6; Bancroft, *History of the United States*, chap. ii, p. 401; and Locke, *Anti-Slavery*, p. 32.

of undesirable persons into the "Body Politick," the Quakers proceeded on the principle that all men are brethren and, being equal before God, should be considered equal before the law. On account of unduly emphasizing the relation of man to God, the Puritans "atrophied their social humanitarian instinct" and developed into a race of self-conscious saints. Be lieving in human nature and laying stress upon the relation between man and man, the Quakers became the friends of all humanity.[4]

In 1693 George Keith, a leading Quaker of his day, came forward as a promoter of the religious training of the slaves as a preparation for emancipation. William Penn advocated the emancipation of slaves, that they might have every opportunity for improvement. In 1695 the Quakers while protesting against the slave trade denounced also the policy of neglecting their moral and spiritual welfare.[5] The growing interest of this sect in the Negroes was shown later by the development in 1713 of a definite scheme for freeing and returning them to Africa after having been educated and trained to serve as missionaries on that continent.

When the manumission of the slaves was checked by the reaction against that class and it

[4] *A Brief Statement of the Rise and Progress of the Testimony of the Quakers,* passim; Woodson, *The Education of the Negro Prior to 1861,* p. 43.

[5] Woodson, *The Education of the Negro Prior to 1861,* p. 44; and Locke, *Anti-Slavery,* p. 32.

became more of a problem to establish them in a hostile environment, certain Quakers of North Carolina and Virginia adopted the scheme of settling them in Northern States.[6] At first, they sent such freedmen to Pennsylvania. But for various reasons this did not prove to be the best asylum. In the first place, Pennsylvania bordered on the slave States, Maryland and Virginia, from which agents came to kidnap free Negroes. Furthermore, too many Negroes were already rushing to that commonwealth as the Negroes' heaven and there was the chance that the Negroes might be settled elsewhere in the North, where they might have better economic opportunities.[7] A committee of forty was accordingly appointed by North Carolina Quakers in 1822 to examine the laws of other free States with a view to determining what section would be most suitable for colonizing these blacks. This committee recommended in its report that the blacks be colonized in Ohio, Indiana and Illinois.

The yearly meeting, therefore, ordered the removal of such Negroes as fast as they were willing or as might be consistent with the profession of their sect, and instructed the agents effecting the removal to draw on the treasury for any sum not exceeding two hundred dollars to defray expenses. An increasing number

[6] *The Southern Workman,* xxxvii, pp. 158–169.

[7] Turner, *The Negro in Pennsylvania,* pp. 144, 145, 151, 155.

reached these States every year but, owing to the inducements offered by the American Colonization Society, some of them went to Liberia. When Liberia, however, developed into every thing but a haven of rest, the number sent to the settlements in the Northwest greatly increased. The quarterly meeting succeeded in sending to the West 133 Negroes, including 23 free blacks and slaves given up because they were connected by marriage with those to be transplanted.[8] The Negro colonists seemed to prefer Indiana.[9] They went in three companies and with suitable young Friends to whom were executed powers of attorney to manumit, set free, settle and bind them out.[10] Thirteen carts and wagons were bought for these three companies; $1,250 was furnished for their traveling expenses and clothing, the whole cost amounting to $2,490. It was planned to send forty or fifty to Long Island and twenty to the interior of Pennsylvania, but they failed to prosper and reports concerning them stamped them as destitute and deplorably ignorant. Those who went to Ohio and Indiana, however, did well.[11]

Later we receive another interesting account of this exodus. David White led a company of fifty-three into the West, thirty-eight of whom

[8] *Southern Workman,* xxxvii, p. 157.

[9] Levi Coffin, *Reminiscences,* chaps. i and ii.

[10] *Southern Workman,* xxxvii, pp. 161–163.

[11] Coffin, *Reminiscences,* p. 109; and Howe's *Historical Collections,* p. 356.

belonged to Friends, five to a member who had ordered that they be taken West at his expense. Six of these slaves belonged to Samuel Lawrence, a Negro slaveholder, who had purchased himself and family. White pathetically reports the case of four of the women who had married slave husbands and had twenty children for the possession of whom the Friends had to stand a lawsuit in the courts. The women had decided to leave their husbands behind but the thought of separation so tormented them that they made an effort to secure their liberty. Upon appealing to their masters for terms the owners, somewhat moved by compassion, sold them for one half of their value. White then went West and left four in Chillicothe, twenty-three in Leesburg and twenty-six in Wayne County, Indiana, without encountering any material difficulty.[12]

Others had thought of this plan but the Quakers actually carried it out on a small scale. Here we see again not only their desire to have the Negroes emancipated but the vital interest of the Quakers in success of the blacks, for members of this sect not only liberated their slaves but sold out their own holdings in the South and moved with these freedmen into the North. Quakers who then lived in free States offered fugitives material assistance by open and clandestine methods.[13] The most prom-

[12] *Southern Workman*, xxxvii, pp. 162, 163.
[13] Levi Coffin, *Reminiscences*, pp. 108–111.

inent leader developed by the movement was Levi Coffin, whose daring deeds in behalf of the fugitives made him the reputed President of the Underground Railroad. Most of the Quaker settlements of Negroes with which he was connected were made in what is now Hamilton, Howard, Wayne, Randolph, Vigo, Gibson, Grant, Rush, and Tipton Counties, Indiana, and Darke County, Ohio.

The promotion of this movement by the Quakers was well on its way by 1815 and was not materially checked until the fifties when the operations of the drastic fugitive slave law interfered, and even then the movement had gained such momentum and the execution of that mischievous measure had produced in the North so much reaction like that expressed in the personal liberty laws, that it could not be stopped. The Negroes found homes in Western New York, Western Pennsylvania and throughout the Northwest Territory. The Negro population of York, Harrisburg and Philadelphia rapidly increased. A settlement of Negroes developed at Sandy Lake in Northwestern Pennsylvania[14] and there was another near Berlin Cross Roads in Ohio.[15] A group of Negroes migrating to this same State found homes in the Van Buren Township of Shelby County.[16] A

---

[14] Siebert, *The Underground Railroad*, p. 249.

[15] Langston, *From the Virginia Plantation to the National Capitol*, p. 35.

[16] Howe, *Historical Collections*, p. 465.

more significant settlement in the State was
made by Samuel Gist, an Englishman possessing extensive plantations in Hanover, Amherst,
and Henrico Counties, Virginia. He provided
in his will that his slaves should be freed and
sent to the North. He further provided that the
revenue from his plantation the last year of his
life be applied in building schoolhouses and
churches for their accommodation, and "that
all money coming to him in Virginia be set
aside for the employment of ministers and
teachers to instruct them." In 1818, Wickham,
the executor of his estate, purchased land and
established these Negroes in what was called
the Upper and Lower Camps of Brown
County.[17]

Augustus Wattles, a Quaker from Connecticut, made a settlement in Mercer County, Ohio,
early in the nineteenth century. In the winter
of 1833–4, he providentially became acquainted
with the colored people of Cincinnati, finding
there about "4,000 totally ignorant of every thing
calculated to make good citizens." As most of
them had been slaves, excluded from every avenue of moral and mental improvement, he established for them a school which he maintained
for two years. He then proposed to these Negroes to go into the country and purchase land to
remove them "from those contaminating influences which had so long crushed them in our

[17] *History of Brown County, Ohio*, p. 313.

cities and villages.''[18]   They consented on the condition that he would accompany them and teach school. He travelled through Canada, Michigan and Indiana, looking for a suitable location, and finally selected for settlement a place in Mercer County, Ohio. In 1835, he made the first purchase of land there for this purpose and before 1838 Negroes had bought there about 30,000 acres, at the earnest appeal of this benefactor, who had travelled into almost every neighborhood of the blacks in the State, and laid before them the benefits of a permanent home for themselves and of education for their children.[19]

This settlement was further increased in 1858 by the manumitted slaves of John Harper of North Carolina.[20]   John Randolph of Roanoke endeavored to establish his slaves as freemen in this county but the Germans who had settled in that community a little ahead of them started

[18] Wattles said: he purchased for himself 190 acres of land, to establish a manual labor school for colored boys. He had maintained a school on it, at his own expense, till the eleventh of November, 1842. While in Philadelphia the winter before, he became acquainted with the trustees of the late Samuel Emlen, a Friend of New Jersey. He left by his will $20,000 for the ''support and education in school learning and the mechanic arts and agriculture, boys, of African and Indian descent, whose parents would give them up to the school. They united their means and purchased Wattles farm, and appointed him the superintendent of the establishment, which they called the Emlen Institute.''—See Howe's *Historical Collections*, p. 356.

[19] Howe's *Historical Collections*, p. 355.

[20] *Manuscripts* in the possession of J. E. Moorland.

such a disturbance that Randolph's executor could not carry out his plan, although he had purchased a large tract of land there.[21] It was necessary to send these freemen to Miami County. Theodoric H. Gregg of Dinwiddie County, Virginia, liberated his slaves in 1854 and sent them to Ohio.[22] Nearer to the Civil War, when public opinion was proscribing the uplift of Negroes in Kentucky, Noah Spears secured near Xenia, Greene County, Ohio, a small parcel of land for sixteen of his former bondsmen in 1856.[23] Other freedmen found their way to this community in later years and it became so prosperous that it was selected as the site of Wilberforce University.

This transplantation extended into Michigan. With the help of persons philanthropically inclined there sprang up a flourishing group of Negroes in Detroit. Early in the nineteenth century they began to acquire property and to provide for the education of their children. Their record was such as to merit the encomiums of their fellow white citizens. In later years this group in Detroit was increased by the operation of laws hostile to free Negroes in the South in that life for this class not only became intolerable but necessitated their expatriation. Because of the Virginia drastic laws and espe-

[21] *The African Repository*, xxii, pp. 322, 333.

[22] Simmons, *Men of Mark*, p. 723.

[23] *Southern Workman*, xxxvii, p. 158.

cially that of 1838 prohibiting the return to that
State of such Negro students as had been accustomed to go North to attend school, after
they were denied this privilege at home, the
father of Richard DeBaptiste and Marie Louis
More, the mother of Fannie M. Richards, led a
colony of free Negroes from Fredericksburg to
Detroit.[24]   And for about similar reasons the
father of Robert A. Pelham conducted others
from Petersburg, Virginia, in 1859.[25]   One
Saunders, a planter of Cabell County, West Virginia, liberated his slaves some years later and
furnished them homes among the Negroes settled in Cass County, Michigan, about ninety
miles east of Chicago, and ninety-five miles
west of Detroit.

This settlement had become attractive to
fugitive slaves and freedmen because the Quakers settled there welcomed them on their way to
freedom and in some cases encouraged them to
remain among them.   When the increase of
fugitives was rendered impossible during the
fifties when the Fugitive Slave Law was being
enforced, there was still a steady growth due
to the manumission of slaves by sympathetic
and benevolent masters in the South.[26]   Most
of these Negroes settled in Calvin Township,
in that county, so that of the 1,376 residing there

24 *The Journal of Negro History*, I, pp. 23–33.
25 *Ibid.*, I, p. 26.
26 *The African Repository*, passim.

in 1860, 795 were established in this district, there being only 580 whites dispersed among them. The Negro settlers did not then obtain control of the government but they early purchased land to the extent of several thousand acres and developed into successful small farmers. Being a little more prosperous than the average Negro community in the North, the Cass County settlement not only attracted Negroes fleeing from hardships in the South but also those who had for some years unsuccessfully endeavored to establish themselves in other communities on free soil.[27]

These settlements were duplicated a little farther west in Illinois. Edward Coles, a Virginian, who in 1818 emigrated to Illinois, of which he later served as Governor and as liberator from slavery, settled his slaves in that

[27] Although constituting a majority of the population even before the Civil War the Negroes of this township did not get recognition in the local government until 1875 when John Allen, a Negro, was elected township treasurer. From that time until about 1890 the Negroes always shared the honors of office with their white citizens and since that time they have usually had entire control of the local government in that township, holding such offices as supervisor, clerk, treasurer, road commissioner, and school director. Their record has been that of efficiency. Boss rule among them is not known. The best man for an office is generally sought; for this is a community of independent farmers. In 1907 one hundred and eleven different farmers in this community had holdings of 10,439 acres. Their township usually has very few delinquent taxpayers and it promptly makes its returns to the county.— See the *Southern Workman*, xxxvii, pp. 486–489.

commonwealth. He brought them to Edwards-
ville, where they constituted a community
known as "Coles' Negroes."[28] There was another community of Negroes in Illinois in what
is now called Brooklyn situated north of East
St. Louis. This town was a center of some
consequence in the thirties. It became a station
of the Underground Railroad on the route to
Alton and to Canada. As all of the Negroes
who emerged from the South did not go farther
into the North, the black population of the town
gradually grew despite the fact that slave
hunters captured and reenslaved many of the
Negroes who settled there.[29]

These settlements together with favorable
communities of sympathetic whites promoted
the migration of the free Negroes and fugitives
from the South by serving as centers offering
assistance to those fleeing to the free States and
to Canada. The fugitives usually found friends
in Philadelphia, Columbia, Pittsburgh, Elmira,
Rochester, Buffalo, Gallipolis, Portsmouth,
Akron, Cincinnati, and Detroit. They passed
on the way to freedom through Columbia, Philadelphia, Elizabethtown and by way of sea to

[28] Davidson and Stowe, *A Complete History of Illinois*, pp.
321, 322; and Washburn, *Edward Coles,* pp. 44 and 53.

[29] The Negro population of this town so rapidly increased
after the war that it has become a Negro town and unfortunately a bad one. Much improvement has been made in
recent years.—See *Southern Workman*, xxxvii, pp. 489–494.

New York and Boston, from which they proceeded to permanent settlements in the North.[30] In the West, the migration of the blacks was further facilitated by the peculiar geographic condition in that the Appalachian highland, extending like a peninsula into the South, had a natural endowment which produced a class of white citizens hostile to the institution of slavery. These mountaineers coming later to the colonies had to go to the hills and mountains because the first comers from Europe had taken up the land near the sea. Being of the German and Scotch-Irish Presbyterian stock, they had ideals differing widely from those of the seaboard slaveholders.[31] The mountaineers believed in "civil liberty in fee simple, and an open road to civil honors, secured to the poorest and feeblest members of society." The eastern element had for their ideal a government of interests for the people. They believed in liberty but that of kings, lords, and commons, not of all the people.[32]

Settled along the Appalachian highland, these new stocks continued to differ from those dwelling near the sea, especially on the slavery question.[33] The natural endowment of the moun-

33 Olmsted, *Back Country*, p. 134.

30 Still, *Underground Railroad*, passim; Siebert, *Underground Railroad*, pp. 34, 35, 40, 42, 43, 48, 56, 59, 62, 64, 70, 145, 147; Drew, *Refugee*, pp. 72, 97, 114, 152, 335 and 373.

31 *The Journal of Negro History*, I, pp. 132–162.

32 *Ibid.*, I, 138.

tainous section made slavery there unprofitable and the mountaineers bore it grievously that they were attached to commonwealths dominated by the radical pro-slavery element of the South, who sacrificed all other interests to safeguard those of the peculiar institution. There developed a number of clashes in all of the legislatures and constitutional conventions of the Southern States along the Atlantic, but in every case the defenders of the interests of slavery won. When, therefore, slaves with the assistance of anti-slavery mountaineers began to escape to the free States, they had little difficulty in making their way through the Appalachian region, where the love of freedom had so set the people against slavery that although some of them yielded to the inevitable sin, they never made any systematic effort to protect it.[34]

The development of the movement in these mountains was more than interesting. During the first quarter of the nineteenth century there

[34] In the Appalachian mountains, however, the settlers were loath to follow the fortunes of the ardent pro-slavery element. Actual abolition, for example, was never popular in western Virginia, but the love of the people of that section for freedom kept them estranged from the slaveholding districts of the State, which by 1850 had completely committed themselves to the pro-slavery propaganda. In the Convention of 1829–30 Upshur said there existed in a great portion of the West (of Virginia) a rooted antipathy to the slave. John Randolph was alarmed at the fanatical spirit on the subject of slavery, which was growing in Virginia.—See the *Journal of Negro History*, I, p. 142.

were many ardent anti-slavery leaders in the
mountains. These were not particularly interested in the Negro but were determined to keep
that soil for freedom that the settlers might
there realize the ideals for which they had left
their homes in Europe. When the industrial
revolution with the attendant rise of the plantation cotton culture made abolition in the
South improbable, some of them became colonizationists, hoping to destroy the institution
through deportation, which would remove the
objection of certain masters who would free
their slaves provided they were not left in the
States to become a public charge.[35] Some of
this sentiment continued in the mountains even
until the Civil War. The highlanders, therefore, found themselves involved in a continuous
embroglio because they were not moved by reactionary influences which were unifying the
South for its bold effort to make slavery a national institution.[36] The other members of the
mountaineer anti-slavery group became attached to the Underground Railroad system, endeavoring by secret methods to place on free
soil a sufficiently large number of fugitives to
show a decided diminution in the South.[37] John
Brown, who communicated with the South
through these mountains, thought that his work

[35] Adams, *Neglected Period of Anti-Slavery.*
[36] *The Journal of Negro History,* I, pp. 132–160.
[37] Siebert, *Underground Railroad,* p. 166.

would be a success, if he could change the situation in one county in each of these States. The lines along which these Underground Railroad operators moved connected naturally with the Quaker settlements established in free States and the favorable sections in the Appalachian region. Many of these workers were Quakers who had already established settlements of slaves on estates which they had purchased in the Northwest Territory. Among these were John Rankin, James Gilliland, Jesse Lockehart, Robert Dobbins, Samuel Crothers, Hugh L. Fullerton, and William Dickey. Thus they connected the heart of the South with the avenues to freedom in the North.[38] There were routes extending from this section into Ohio, Indiana, Illinois and Pennsylvania. Over the Ohio and Kentucky route culminating chiefly in Cleveland, Sandusky and Detroit, however, more fugitives made their way to freedom than through any other avenue,[39] partly too because they found the limestone caves very helpful for hiding by day. These operations extended even through Tennessee into northern Georgia and Alabama. Dillingham, Josiah Henson and Harriet Tubman used these routes to deliver many a Negro from slavery.

The opportunity thus offered to help the oppressed brought forward a class of anti-slavery men, who went beyond the limit of merely ex-

[38] Adams, *Neglected Period of Anti-Slavery.*
[39] Siebert, *Underground Railroad*, chaps. v and vi.

pressing their horror of the evil. They believed that something should be done "to deliver the poor that cry and to direct the wanderer in the right way."[40] Translating into action what had long been restricted to academic discussion, these philanthropic workers ushered in a new era in the uplift of the blacks, making abolition more of a reality. The abolition element of the North then could no longer be considered an insignificant minority advocating a hopeless cause but a factor in drawing from the South a part of its slave population and at the same time offering asylum to the free Negroes whom the southerners considered undesirable.[41] Prominent among those who aided this migration in various ways were Benjamin Lundy of Tennessee and James G. Birney, a former slaveholder of Huntsville, Alabama, who manumitted his slaves and apprenticed and educated some of them in Ohio.

This exodus of the Negroes to the free States promoted the migration of others of their race to Canada, a more congenial part beyond the borders of the United States. The movement from the free States into Canada, moreover, was contemporary with that from the South to the free States as will be evidenced by the fact that 15,000 of the 60,000 Negroes in Canada in 1860 were free born. As Detroit was the chief

---

[40] *An Address to the People of North Carolina on the Evils of Slavery.*

[41] Washington, *Story of the Negro,* I, chaps. xii, xiii and xiv.

gateway for them to Canada, most of these refugees settled in towns of Southern Ontario not far from that city. These were Dawn, Colchester, Elgin, Dresden, Windsor, Sandwich, Bush, Wilberforce, Hamilton, St. Catherines, Chatham, Riley, Anderton, London, Malden and Gonfield.[42] And their coming to Canada was not checked even by request from their enemies that they be turned away from that country as undesirables, for some of the white people there welcomed and assisted them. Canadians later experienced a change in their attitude toward these refugees but these British Americans never made the life of the Negro there so intolerable as was the case in some of the free States.

It should be observed here that this movement, unlike the exodus of the Negroes of to-day, affected an unequal distribution of the enlightened Negroes.[43] Those who are fleeing from the South to-day are largely laborers seeking economic opportunities. The motive at work in the mind of the antebellum refugee was higher. In 1840 there were more intelligent blacks in the South than in the North but not so after 1850, despite the vigorous execution of the Fugitive Slave Law in some parts of the North. While the free Negro population of the slave

[42] *Father Henson's Story of his own Life*, p. 209; Coffin, *Reminiscences*, pp. 247–256; Howe, *The Refugees from Slavery*, p. 77; Haviland, *A Woman's Work*, pp. 192, 193, 196.

[43] Woodson, *The Education of the Negro Prior to 1861*, pp. 236–240.

States increased only 23,736 from 1850 to 1860, that of the free States increased 29,839. In the South, only Delaware, Maryland and North Carolina showed a noticeable increase in the number of free persons of color during the decade immediately preceding the Civil War. This element of the population had only slightly increased in Alabama, Kentucky, Missouri, Tennessee, Virginia, Louisiana, South Carolina and the District of Columbia. The number of free Negroes of Florida remained constant. Those of Arkansas, Mississippi and Texas diminished. In the North, of course, the migration had caused the tendency to be in the other direction. With the exception of Maine, New Hampshire, Vermont and New York which had about the same free colored population in 1860 as they had in 1850 there was a general increase in the number of Negroes in the free States. Ohio led in this respect, having had during this period an increase of 11,394.[44] A glance at the table on the accompanying page will show in detail the results of this migration.

STATISTICS OF THE FREE COLORED POPULATION OF THE UNITED STATES

State	Population	
	1850	1860
Alabama	2,265	2,690
Arkansas	608	144
California	962	4,086
Connecticut	7,693	8,627
Delaware	18,073	19,829

44 *The United States Censuses of 1850 and 1860.*

Florida	932	932
Georgia	2,931	3,500
Illinois	5,436	7,628
Indiana	11,262	11,428
Iowa	333	1,069
Kentucky	10,011	10,684
Louisiana	17,462	18,647
Maine	1,356	1,327
Kansas		625
Maryland	74,723	83,942
Massachusetts	9,064	9,602
Michigan	2,583	6,797
Minnesota		259
Mississippi	930	773
Missouri	2,618	3,572
New Hampshire	520	494
New Jersey	23,810	25,318
New York	49,069	49,005
North Carolina	27,463	30,463
Ohio	25,279	36,673
Oregon		128
Pennsylvania	53,626	56,949
Rhode Island	3,670	3,952
South Carolina	8,960	9,914
Tennessee	6,422	7,300
Texas	397	355
Vermont	718	709
Virginia	54,333	58,042
Wisconsin	635	1,171
Territories:		
Colorado		46
Dakota		0
District of Columbia	10,059	11,131
Minnesota	39	
Nebraska		67
Nevada		45
New Mexico	207	85
Oregon	24	
Utah	22	30
Washington		30
Total	434,495	488,070

CHAPTER III

FIGHTING IT OUT ON FREE SOIL

HOW, then, was this increasing influx of refugees from the South to be received in the free States? In the older Northern States where there could be no danger of an Africanization of a large district, the coming of the Negroes did not cause general excitement, though at times the feeling in certain localities was sufficient to make one think so.[1] Fearing that the immigration of the Negroes into the North might so increase their numbers as to make them constitute a rather important part in the community, however, some free States enacted laws to restrict the privileges of the blacks.

Free Negroes had voted in all the colonies except Georgia and South Carolina, if they had the property qualification; but after the sentiment attendant upon the struggle for the rights of man had passed away there set in a reaction.[2] Delaware, Maryland, Virginia and Kentucky disfranchised all Negroes not long after the Revolution. They voted in North Carolina until

[1] *The New York Daily Advertiser,* Sept. 22, 1800; *The New York Journal of Commerce,* July 12, 1834; and *The New York Commercial Advertiser,* July 12, 1834.

[2] Hart, *Slavery and Abolition,* pp. 53, 82.

1835, when the State, feeling that this privilege of one class of Negroes might affect the enslavement of the other, prohibited it. The Northern States, following in their wake, set up the same barriers against the blacks. They were disfranchised in New Jersey in 1807, in Connecticut in 1814, and in Pennsylvania in 1838. In 1811 New York passed an act requiring the production of certificates of freedom from blacks or mulattoes offering to vote. The second constitution, adopted in 1823, provided that no man of color, unless he had been for three years a citizen of that State and for one year next preceding any election, should be seized and possessed of a freehold estate, should be allowed to vote, although this qualification was not required of the whites. An act of 1824 relating to the government of the Stockbridge Indians provided that no Negro or mulatto should vote in their councils.[3]

That increasing prejudice was to a great extent the result of the immigration into the North of Negroes in the rough, was nowhere better illustrated than in Pennsylvania. Prior to 1800, and especially after 1780, when the State provided for gradual emancipation, there was little race prejudice in Pennsylvania.[4] When the re-

[3] Goodell, *American Slave Code*, Part III, chap. i; Hurd, *The Law of Freedom and Bondage*, I, pp. 51, 61, 67, 81, 89, 101, 111; Woodson, *The Education of the Negro Prior to 1861*, pp. 151–178.

[4] Benezet, *Short Observations*, p. 12.

actionary legislation of the South made life
intolerable for the Negroes, debasing them to
the plane of beasts, many of the free people of
color from Virginia, Maryland and Delaware
moved or escaped into Pennsylvania like a
steady stream during the next sixty years. As
these Negroes tended to concentrate in towns
and cities, they caused the supply of labor to exceed the demand, lowering the wages of some
and driving out of employment a number of
others who became paupers and consequently
criminals. There set in too an intense struggle
between the black and white laborers,[5] im-
mensely accelerating the growth of race prejudice, especially when the abolitionists and
Quakers were giving Negroes industrial training.

The first exhibition of this prejudice was seen
among the lower classes of white people, largely
Irish and Germans, who, devoted to menial
labor, competed directly with the Negroes. It
did not require a long time, however, for this
feeling to react on the higher classes of whites
where Negroes settled in large groups. A
strong protest arose from the menace of Negro
paupers. An attempt was made in 1804 to compel free Negroes to maintain those that might
become a public charge.[6] In 1813 the mayor,
aldermen and citizens of Philadelphia asked

[5] Turner, *The Negro in Pennsylvania*, pp. 143–145.
[6] *Journal of House*, 1823–24, p. 824.

that free Negroes be taxed to support their poor.[7] Two Philadelphia representatives in the Pennsylvania Legislature had a committee appointed in 1815 to consider the advisability of preventing the immigration of Negroes.[8] One of the causes then at work there was that the black population had recently increased to four thousand in Philadelphia and more than four thousand others had come into the city since the previous registration.

They were arriving much faster than they could be assimilated. The State of Pennsylvania had about exterminated slavery by 1840, having only 40 slaves that year and only a few hundred at any time after 1810. Many of these, of course, had not had time to make their way in life as freedmen. To show how much the rapid migration to that city aggravated the situation under these circumstances one needs but note the statistics of the increase of the free people of color in that State. There were only 22,492 such persons in Pennsylvania in 1810, but in 1820 there were 30,202, and in 1830 as many as 37,930. This number increased to 47,854 by 1840, to 53,626 by 1850, and to 56,949 by 1860. The undesirable aspect of the situation was that most of the migrating blacks came in crude form.[9] ''On arriving,'' therefore, says a contemporary, ''they abandoned them-

[7] *Journal of House*, 1812–1813, pp. 481, 482.

[8] *Ibid.*, 1814–1815, p. 101.

[9] *United States Censuses*, 1790–1860.

selves to all manner of debauchery and dissipation to the great annoyance of many citizens.''[10]

Thereafter followed a number of clashes developing finally into a series of riots of a grave nature. Innocent Negroes, attacked at first for purposes of sport and later for sinister designs, were often badly beaten in the streets or even cut with knives. The offenders were not punished and if the Negroes defended themselves they were usually severely penalized. In 1819 three white women stoned a woman of color to death.[11] A few youths entered a Negro church in Philadelphia in 1825 and by throwing pepper to give rise to suffocating fumes caused a panic which resulted in the death of several Negroes.[12] When the citizens of New Haven, Connecticut, arrayed themselves in 1831 against the plan to establish in that city a Negro manual labor college, there was held in Philadelphia a meeting which passed resolutions enthusiastically endorsing this effort to rid the community of the evil of the immigration of free Negroes. There arose also the custom of driving Negroes away from Independence Square on the Fourth of July because they were neither considered nor desired as a part of the body politic.[13]

[10] Brannagan, *Serious Remonstrances*, p. 68.

[11] Turner, *The Negro in Pennsylvania*, p. 145; *The Philadelphia Gazette*, June 30, 1819.

[12] *Democratic Press, Philadelphia Gazette*, Nov. 21, 1825.

[13] Turner, *The Negro in Pennsylvania*, p. 146.

It was thought that in the state of feeling of the thirties that the Negro would be annihilated. De Tocqueville also observed that the Negroes were more detested in the free States than in those where they were held as slaves.[14] There had been such a reaction since 1800 that no positions of consequence were open to Negroes, however well educated they might be, and the education of the blacks which was once vigorously prosecuted there became unpopular.[15] This was especially true of Harrisburg and Philadelphia but by no means confined to large cities. The Philadelphia press said nothing in behalf of the race. It was generally thought that freedom had not been an advantage to the Negro and that instead of making progress they had filled jails and almshouses and multiplied pest holes to afflict the cities with disease and crime.

The Negroes of York carefully worked out in 1803 a plan to burn the city. Incendiaries set on fire a number of houses, eleven of which were destroyed, whereas there were other attempts at a general destruction of the city. The authorities arrested a number of Negroes but ran the risk of having the jail broken open by their sympathizing fellowmen. After a reign of terror for half a week, order was restored and twenty of the accused were convicted of arson.

[14] De Tocqueville, *Democracy in America,* II, pp. 292, 294.
[15] Turner, *The Negro in Pennsylvania,* p. 148.

In 1820 there occurred so many conflagrations
that a vigilance committee was organized.[16]
Whether or not the Negroes were guilty of the
crime is not known but numbers of them left
either on account of the fear of punishment or
because of the indignities to which they were
subjected. Numerous petitions, therefore, came
before the legislature to stop the immigration of
Negroes. It was proposed in 1840 to tax all free
Negroes to assist them in getting out of the
State for colonization.[17]   The citizens of Lehigh
County asked the authorities in 1830 to expel
all Negroes and persons of color found in the
State.[18]   Another petition prayed that they be
deprived of the freedom of movement. Bills
embodying these ideas were frequently considered but they were never passed.

Stronger opposition than this, however, was
manifested in the form of actual outbreaks on a
large scale in Philadelphia. The immediate
cause of this first real clash was the abolition
agitation in the city in 1834 following the exciting news of other such disturbances a few
months prior to this date in several northern
cities. A group of boys started the riot by destroying a Negro resort. A mob then proceeded
to the Negro district, where white and colored
men engaged in a fight with clubs and stones.

---

[16] Turner, *The Negro in Pennsylvania*, pp. 152, 153.

[17] *African Repository*, VIII, pp. 125, 283; *Journal of House*,
1840, I, pp. 347, 508, 614, 622, 623, 680.

[18] *Journal of Senate*, 1850, I, pp. 454, 479.

The next day the mob ruined the African Presbyterian Church and attacked some Negroes, destroying their property and beating them mercilessly. This riot continued for three days. A committee appointed to inquire into the causes of the riot reported that the aim of the rioters had been to make the Negroes go away because it was believed that their labor was depriving them of work and because the blacks had shielded criminals and had made such noise and disorder in their churches as to make them a nuisance. It seemed that the most intelligent and well-to-do people of Philadelphia keenly felt it that the city had thus been disgraced, but the mob spirit continued.[19]

The very next year was marked by the same sort of disorder. Because a half-witted Negro attempted to murder a white man, a large mob stirred up the city again. There was a repetition of the beating of Negroes and of the destruction of property while the police, as the year before, were so inactive as to give rise to the charge that they were accessories to the riot.[20] In 1838 there occurred another outbreak which developed into an anti-abolition riot, as the public mind had been much exercised by the discussions of abolitionists and by their close social contact with the Negroes. The clash came

[19] This is well narrated in Turner's *Negro in Pennsylvania,* p. 160, and in Du Bois's *The Philadelphia Negro,* p. 27.

[20] Turner, *The Negro in Pennsylvania,* pp. 161, 162.

on the seventeenth of May when Pennsylvania Hall, the center of abolition agitation, was burned. Fighting between the blacks and whites ensued the following night when the Colored Orphan Asylum was attacked and a Negro church burned. Order was finally restored for the good of all concerned, but that a majority of the people sympathized with the rioters was evidenced by the fact that the committee charged with investigating the disturbance reported that the mob was composed of strangers who could not be recognized.[21] It is well to note here that this riot occurred the year the Negroes in Pennsylvania were disfranchised.

Following the example of Philadelphia, Pittsburgh had a riot in 1839 resulting in the maltreatment of a number of Negroes and the demolishing of some of their houses. When the Negroes of Philadelphia paraded the city in 1842, celebrating the abolition of slavery in the West Indies, there ensued a battle led by the whites who undertook to break up the procession. Along with the beating and killing of the usual number went also the destruction of the New African Hall and the Negro Presbyterian church. The grand jury charged with the inquiry into the causes reported that the procession was to be blamed. For several years thereafter the city remained quiet until 1849 when there occurred a raid on the blacks by the *Killers*

21 Turner, *The Negro in Pennsylvania*, pp. 162, 163.

of Moyamensing, using firearms with which
many were wounded. This disturbance was
finally quelled by aid of the militia.[22]
These clashes sometimes reached farther
north than the free States bordering on the
slave commonwealths. Mobs broke up abolition meetings in the city of New York in 1834
when there were sent to Congress numerous petitions for the abolition of slavery. This mob
even assailed such eminent citizens as Arthur
and Lewis Tappan, mainly on account of their
friendly attitude toward the Negroes.[23] On October 21, 1834, the same feeling developed in
Utica, where was to be held an anti-slavery
meeting according to previous notice. The six
hundred delegates who assembled there were
warned to disband. A mob then organized itself
and drove the delegates from the town. That
same month the people of Palmyra, New York,
held a meeting at which they adopted resolutions to the effect that owners of houses or tenements in that town occupied by blacks of the
character complained of be requested to use all
their rightful means to clear their premises of
such occupants at the earliest possible period;
and that it be recommended that such proprietors refuse to rent the same thereafter to
any person of color whatever.[24]   In New York

[22] Turner, *The Negro in Pennsylvania,* p. 163; and *The
Liberator,* July 4, 1835.
[23] *The Liberator,* Oct. 24, 1834.
[24] *Ibid.,* October 24, 1834.

Negroes were excluded from places of amusement and public conveyances and segregated in places of worship. In the draft riots which occurred there in 1863, one of the aims of the mobs was to assassinate Negroes and to destroy their property. They burned the Colored Orplan Asylum of that city and hanged Negroes to lamp-posts.

The situation in parts of New England was not much better. For fear of the evils of an increasing population of free persons of color the people of Canaan, New Hampshire, broke up the Noyes Academy because it decided to admit Negro students, thinking that many of the race might thereby be encouraged to come to that State.[25] When Prudence Crandall established in Canterbury, Connecticut, an academy to which she decided to admit Negroes, the mayor, selectmen and citizens of the city protested, and when their protests failed to deter this heroine, they induced the legislature to enact a special law covering the case and invoked the measure to have Prudence Crandall imprisoned because she would not desist.[26] This very

[25] Jay, *An Inquiry*, pp. 28–29.

[26] *An Act in Addition to an Act for the Admission and Settlement of Inhabitants of Towns.*

1. Whereas attempts have been made to establish literary institutions in this State for the instruction of colored people belonging to other States and countries, which would tend to the great increase of the colored population of the State, and thereby to the injury of the people, therefore;

law and the arguments upholding it justified the drastic measure on the ground that an increase

Be it resolved that no person shall set up or establish in this State, any school, academy, or literary institution for the instruction or education of colored persons, who are not inhabitants of this State, nor instruct or teach in any school, academy, or other literary institution whatever in this State, or harbor or board for the purpose of attending or being taught or instructed in any such school, academy, or other literary institution, any person who is not an inhabitant of any town in this State, without the consent in writing, first obtained of a majority of the civil authority, and also of the selectmen of the town in which such schools, academy, or literary institution is situated; and each and every person who shall knowingly do any act forbidden as aforesaid, or shall be aiding or assisting therein, shall for the first offense forfeit and pay to the treasurer of this State a fine of one hundred dollars and for the second offense shall forfeit and pay a fine of two hundred dollars, and so double for every offense of which he or she shall be convicted. And all informing officers are required to make due presentment of all breaches of this act. Provided that nothing in this act shall extend to any district school established in any school society under the laws of this State or to any incorporated school for instruction in this State.

2. Any colored person not an inhabitant of this State who shall reside in any town therein for the purpose of being instructed as aforesaid, may be removed in the manner prescribed in the sixth and seventh sections of the act to which this is an addition.

3. Any person not an inhabitant of this State who shall reside in any town therein for the purpose of being instructed as aforesaid, shall be an admissible witness in all prosecutions under the first section of this act, and may be compelled to give testimony therein, notwithstanding anything in this act, or in the act last aforesaid.

4. That so much of the seventh section of this act to which this is an addition as may provide for the infliction of corporal punishment, be and the same is hereby repealed.—See Hurd's *Law of Freedom and Bondage*, II, pp. 45–46.

in the colored population would be an injury to the people of that State. In the new commonwealths formed out of western territory, there was the same fear as to Negro domination and consequently there followed the wave of legislation intended in some cases not only to withhold from the Negro settlers the exercise of the rights of citizenship but to discourage and even to prevent them from coming into their territory.[27] The question as to what should be done with the Negro was early an issue in Ohio. It came up in the constitutional convention of 1803, and provoked some discussion, but that body considered it sufficient to settle the matter for the time being by merely leaving the Negroes, Indians and foreigners out of the pale of the newly organized body politic by conveniently incorporating the word white throughout the constitution.[28] It was soon evident, however, that the matter had not been settled, and the legislature of 1804 had to give serious consideration to the immigration of Negroes into that State. It was, therefore, enacted that no Negro or mulatto should remain there permanently, unless he could furnish a certificate of freedom issued by some court, that all Negroes in that commonwealth should be regis-

[27] So many Negroes working on the rivers between the slave and free States helped fugitives to escape that there arose a clamor for the discourage of colored employees.

[28] *Constitution of Ohio*, article I, sections 2, 6. *The Journal of Negro History*, I, p. 2.

tered before the following June, and that no
man should employ a Negro who failed to comply with these conditions. Should one be de-
tected in hiring, harboring or hindering the capture of a fugitive black, he was liable to a fine
of $50 and his master could recover pay for the
service of his slave to the amount of fifty cents
a day.[29]

As this legislature did not meet the demands
of those who desired further to discourage
Negro immigration, the Legislature of 1807 was
induced to enact a law to the effect that no Negro
should be permitted to settle in Ohio, unless he
could within 20 days give a bond to the amount
of $500 for his good behavior and assurance that
he would not become a public charge. This
measure provided also for raising the fine for
concealing a fugitive from $50 to $100, one half
of which should go to the person upon the testimony of whom the conviction should be secured.[30]   Negro evidence in a case to which a
white was a party was declared illegal. In 1830
Negroes were excluded from service in the State
militia, in 1831 they were deprived of the privilege of serving on juries, and in 1838 they were
denied the right of having their children educated at the expense of the State.[31]

In Indiana the situation was worse than in

29 *Laws of Ohio*, II, p. 53.
30 *Laws of Ohio*, V, p. 53.
31 Hitchcock, *The Negro in Ohio*, pp. 41, 42.

Ohio. We have already noted above how the settlers in the southern part endeavored to make that a slave State. When that had, after all but being successful, seemed impossible the State enacted laws to prevent or discourage the influx of free Negroes and to restrict the privileges of those already there. In 1824 a stringent law for the return of fugitives was passed.[32] The expulsion of free Negroes was a matter of concern and in 1831 it was provided that unless they could give bond for their behavior and support they could be removed. Otherwise the county overseers could hire out such Negroes to the highest bidder.[33] Negroes were not allowed to attend schools maintained at the public expense, might not give evidence against a white man and could not intermarry with white persons. They might, however, serve as witnesses against Negroes.[34]

In the same way the free Negroes met discouragement in Illinois. They suffered from all the disabilities imposed on their class in Ohio and Indiana and were denied the right to sue for their liberty in the courts. When there arose many abolitionists who encouraged the coming of the fugitives from labor in the South, one element of the citizens of Illinois unwilling to accept this unusual influx of members of an-

---

[32] *Revised Laws of Indiana*, 1831, p. 278.

[33] Perkins, *A Digest of the Declaration of the Supreme Court of Indiana*, p. 590. *Laws of 1853*, p. 60.

[34] Gavin and Hord, *Indiana Revised Statutes*, 1862, p. 452.

other race passed the drastic law of 1853 prohibiting the immigration. It provided for the
prosecution of any person bringing a Negro into
the State and also for arresting and fining any
Negro $50, should he appear there and remain
longer than ten days. If he proved to be unable
to pay the fine, he could be sold to any person
who could pay the cost of the trial.[35]

In Michigan the situation was a little better
but, with the waves of hostile legislation then
sweeping over the new[36] commonwealths, Michigan was not allowed to constitute altogether
an exception. Some of this intense feeling
found expression in the form of a law hostile to
the Negro, this being the act of 1827, which provided for the registration of all free persons of
color and for the exclusion from the territory of
all blacks who could not produce a certificate to
the effect that they were free. Free persons of
color were also required to file bonds with one
or more freehold sureties in the penal sum of
$500 for their good behavior, and the bondsmen

[35] *Illinois Statutes*, 1853, sections 1–4, p. 8.

[36] In 1760 there were both African and Pawnee slaves in
Detroit, 96 of them in 1773 and 175 in 1782. The usual effort
to have slavery legalized was made in 1773. There were seven-
teen slaves in Detroit in 1810 held by virtue of the exceptions
made under the British rule prior to the ratification of Jay's
treaty. Advertisements of runaway slaves appeared in Detroit
papers as late as 1827. Furthermore, there were thirty-two
slaves in Michigan in 1830 but by 1836 all had died or had
been manumitted.—See Farmer, *History of Detroit and Michigan*, I, p. 344.

were expected to provide for their maintenance, if they failed to support themselves. Failure to comply with this law meant expulsion from the territory.[37]

The opposition to the Negroes immigrating into the new West was not restricted to the enactment of laws which in some cases were never enforced. Several communities took the law into their own hands. During these years when the Negroes were seeking freedom in the Northwest Territory and when free blacks were being established there by philanthropists, it seemed to the southern uplanders fleeing from slavery in the border States and foreigners seeking fortunes in the new world that they might possibly be crowded out of this new territory by the Negroes. Frequent clashes, therefore, followed after they had passed through a period of toleration and dependence on the execution of the hostile laws. The clashes of the greatest consequences occurred in the Northwest Territory where a larger number of uplanders from the South had gone, some to escape the ill effects of slavery, and others to hold slaves if possible, and when that seemed impossible, to exclude the blacks altogether.[38] This persecution of the Negroes received also the hearty co-

[37] *Laws of Michigan*, 1827; and Campbell, *Political History of Michigan*, p. 246.

[38] *Proceedings of the Ohio Anti-Slavery Convention*, 1835, p. 19.

operation of the foreign element, who, being an undeveloped class, had to do menial labor in competition with the blacks. The feeling of the foreigners was especially mischievous for the reasons that they were, like the Negroes, at first settled in large numbers in urban communities. Generally speaking, the feeling was like that exhibited by the Germans in Mercer County, Ohio. The citizens of this frontier community, in registering their protest against the settling of Negroes there, adopted the following resolutions:

Resolved, That we will not live among Negroes, as we have settled here first, we have fully determined that we will resist the settlement of blacks and mulattoes in this county to the full extent of our means, the bayonet not excepted.

Resolved, That the blacks of this county be, and they are hereby respectfully requested to leave the country on or before the first day of March, 1847; and in the case of their neglect or refusal to comply with this request, we pledge ourselves to *remove them, peacefully if we can, forcibly if we must.*

Resolved, That we who are here assembled, pledge ourselves not to employ or trade with any black or mulatto person, in any manner whatever, or permit them to have any grinding done at our mills, after the first day of January next.[39]

In 1827 there arose a storm of protest on the occasion of the settling of seventy freedmen in

[39] *African Repository,* XXIII, p. 70.

Lawrence County, Ohio, by a philanthropic master of Pittsylvania County, Virginia.[40] On *Black Friday*, January 1, 1830, eighty Negroes were driven out of Portsmouth, Ohio, at the request of one or two hundred white citizens set forth in an urgent memorial.[41] So many Negroes during these years concentrated at Cincinnati that the laboring element forced the execution of the almost dead law requiring free Negroes to produce certificates and give bonds for their behavior and support.[42] A mob attacked the homes of the blacks, killed a number of them, and forced twelve hundred others to leave for Canada West, where they established the settlement known as Wilberforce.

In 1836 another mob attacked and destroyed there the press of James G. Birney, the editor of the *Philanthropist*, because of the encouragement his abolitionist organ gave to the immigrating Negroes.[43] But in 1841 came a decidedly systematic effort on the part of foreigners and proslavery sympathizers to kill off and drive out the Negroes who were becoming too well established in that city and who were giving offense to white men who desired to deal with them as Negroes were treated in the South. The city continued in this excited state for about a week. There were brought into play in the

[40] *Ohio State Journal*, May 3, 1827.
[41] Evans, *A History of Sciote County, Ohio*, p. 643.
[42] *African Repository*, V, p. 185.
[43] Howe, *Historical Collections*, pp. 225–226.

upheaval the police of the city and the State
militia before the shooting of the Negroes and
burning of their homes could be checked. So
far as is known, no white men were punished,
although a few of them were arrested. Some
Negroes were committed to prison during the
fray. They were thereafter either discharged
upon producing certificates of nativity or giving
bond or were indefinitely held.[44]

In southern Indiana and Illinois the same
condition obtained. Observing the situation in
Indiana, a contributor of *Niles Register* re-
marked, in 1818, upon the arrival there of sixty
or seventy liberated Negroes sent by the society
of Friends of North Carolina, that they were a
species of population that was not acceptable to
the people of that State, ''nor indeed to any
other, whether free or slaveholding, for they cannot rise and become like other men, unless in
countries where their own color predominates,
but must always remain a degraded and inferior
class of persons without the hope of much bet-
tering their condition.''[45]

The *Indiana Farmer,* voicing the sentiment
of that same community, regretted the increase
of this population that seemed to be enlarging
the number sent to that territory. The editor
insisted that the community which enjoys the

[44] *Ibid.,* p. 226, and *The Cincinnati Daily Gazette,* Sept. 14,
1841.

[45] *Niles Register,* XXX, 416.

benefits of the blacks' labor should also suffer all the consequences. Since the people of Indiana derived no advantage from slavery, he begged that they be excused from its inconveniences. Most of the blacks that migrated there, moreover, possessed, thought he, "feelings quite unprepared to make good citizens. A sense of inferiority early impressed on their minds, destitute of every thing but bodily power and having no character to lose, and no prospect of acquiring one, even did they know its value, they are prepared for the commission of any act, when the prospect of evading punishment is favorable."[46]

With the exception of such centers as Eden, Upper Alton, Bellville and Chicago, this antagonistic attitude was general also in the State of Illinois. The Negroes were despised, abused and maltreated as persons who had no rights that the white man should respect. Even in Detroit, Michigan, in 1833 a fracas was started by an attack on Negroes. Because a courageous group of them had effected the rescue and escape of one Thornton Blackburn and his wife who had been arrested by the sheriff as alleged fugitives from Kentucky, the citizens invoked the law of 1827, to require free Negroes to produce a certificate and furnish bonds for their behavior and support.[47] The anti-slavery sentiment there,

[46] *Niles Register*, XXX, 416; *African Repository*, III, p. 25.
[47] Farmer, *History of Detroit and Michigan*, I, chap. 48.

however, was so strong that the law was not long rigidly enforced.⁴⁸   And so it was in several other parts of the West which, however, were exceptional.⁴⁹

⁴⁸ There was the usual effort to have slavery legalized in Michigan. At the time of the fire in 1805 there were six colored men and nine colored women in the town of Detroit. In 1807 there were so many of them that Governor Hull organized a company of colored militia. Joseph Campan owned ten at one time. The importation of slaves was discontinued after September 17, 1792, by act of the Canadian Parliament which provided also that all born thereafter should be free at the age of twenty-five. The Ordinance of 1787 had by its sixth article prohibited it.

⁴⁹ In 1836 a colored man traveling in the West to Cleveland said:

"I have met with good treatment at every place on my journey, even better than what I expected under present circumstances. I will relate an incident that took place on board the steamboat, which will give an idea of the kind treatment with which I have met. When I took the boat at Erie, it being rainy and somewhat disagreeable, I took a cabin passage, to which the captain had not the least objection. When dinner was announced, I intended not to go to the first table but the mate came and urged me to take a seat. I accordingly did and was called upon to carve a large saddle of beef which was before me. This I performed accordingly to the best of my ability. No one of the company manifested any objection or seemed anyways disturbed by my presence."—Extract of a letter from a colored gentleman traveling to the West, Cleveland, Ohio, August 11, 1836.—See *The Philanthropist*, Oct. 21, 1836.

CHAPTER IV

COLONIZATION AS A REMEDY FOR MIGRATION

BECAUSE of these untoward circumstances consequent to the immigration of free Negroes and fugitives into the North, their enemies, and in some cases their well-intentioned friends, advocated the diversion of these elements to foreign soil. Benezet and Brannagan had the idea of settling the Negroes on the public lands in the West largely to relieve the situation in the North.[1] Certain anti-slavery men of Kentucky, as we have observed, recommended the same. But this was hardly advocated at all by the farseeing white men after the close of the first quarter of the nineteenth century. It was by that time very clear that white men would want to occupy all lands within the present limits of the United States. Few statesmen dared to encourage migration to Canada because the large number of fugitives who had already escaped there had attached to that region the stigma of being an asylum for fugitives from the slave States.

The most influential people who gave thought to this question finally decided that the colonization of the Negro in Africa was the only solu-

[1] *The African Repository*, XVI, p. 22.

tion of the problem. The plan of African colonization appealed more generally to the people of both North and South than the other efforts, which, at best, could do no more than to offer local or temporary relief. The African colonizationists proceeded on the basis that the Negroes had no chance for racial development in this country. They could secure no kind of honorable employment, could not associate with congenial white friends whose minds and pursuits might operate as a stimulus upon their industry and could not rise to the level of the successful professional or business men found around them. In short, they must ever be hewers of wood and drawers of water.[2]

To emphasize further the necessity of emigration to Africa the advocates of deportation to foreign soil generally referred to the condition of the migrating Negroes as a case in evidence. "So long," said one, "as you must sit, stand, walk, ride, dwell, eat and sleep *here* and the Negro *there,* he cannot be free in any part of the country."[3] This idea working through the minds of northern men, who had for years thought merely of the injustice of slavery, began to change their attitude toward the abolitionists who had never undertaken to solve the problem of the blacks who were seeking refuge

[2] *The African Repository,* XVI, p. 23; Alexander, *A History of Colonization,* p. 347.

[3] *Ibid.,* XVI, p. 113.

in the North. Many thinkers controlling public opinion then gave audience to the colonizationists and circles once closed to them were thereafter opened.[4] There was, therefore, a tendency toward a more systematic effort than had hitherto characterized the endeavors of the colonizationists. The objects of their philanthropy were not to be stolen away and hurried off to an uncongenial land for the oppressed. They were in accordance with the exigencies of their new situation to be prepared by instruction in mechanic arts, agriculture, science and Biblical literature that some might lead in the higher pursuits and others might skilfully serve their fellows.[5] Private enterprise was at first depended on to carry out the schemes but it soon became evident that a better method was necessary. Finally out of the proposals of various thinkers and out of the actual colonization feats of Paul Cuffé, a Negro, came a national meeting for this purpose, held in Washington, December, 1816, and the organization of the American Colonization Society. This meeting was attended by some of the most prominent men in the United States, among whom were Henry Clay, Francis S. Key, Bishop William Meade, John Randolph and Judge Bushrod Washington.

[4] Jay, *An Inquiry*, pp. 25, 29; Hodgkin, *An Inquiry*, p. 31.
[5] *The African Repository*, IV, p. 276; Griffin, *A Plea for Africa*, p. 65.

The American Colonization Society, however, failed to facilitate the movement of the free Negro from the South and did not promote the general welfare of the race. The reasons for these failures are many. In the first place, the society was all things to all men. To the anti-slavery man whose ardor had been dampened by the meagre results obtained by his agitation, the scheme was the next best thing to remove the objections of slaveholders who had said they would emancipate their bondsmen, if they could be assured of their being deported to foreign soil. To the radical proslavery man and to the northerner hating the Negro it was well adapted to rid the country of the free persons of color whom they regarded as the pariahs of society.[6] Furthermore, although the Colonization Society became seemingly popular and the various States organized branches of it and raised money to promote the movement, the slaveholders as a majority never reached the position of parting with their slaves and the country would not take such radical action as to compel free Negroes to undergo expatriation when militant abolitionists were fearlessly denouncing the scheme.[7]

The free people of color themselves were not only not anxious to go but bore it grievously

[6] Jay, *An Inquiry*, passim; *The Journal of Negro History*, I, pp. 276–301; and Stebbins, *Facts and Opinions*, pp. 200–201.

[7] Hart, *Slavery and Abolition*, p. 237.

that any one should even suggest that they
should be driven from the country in which they
were born and for the independence of which
their fathers had died. They held indignation
meetings throughout the North to denounce the
scheme as a selfish policy inimical to the interests of the people of color.[8] Branded thus as
the inveterate foe of the blacks both slave and
free, the American Colonization Society effected
the deportation of only such Negroes as southern masters felt disposed to emancipate from
time to time and a few others induced to go. As
the industrial revolution early changed the aspect of the economic situation in the South so
as to make slavery seemingly profitable, few
masters ever thought of liberating their slaves.

Scarcely any intelligent Negroes except those
who, for economic or religious reasons were interested, availed themselves of this opportunity
to go to the land of their ancestors. From the
reports of the Colonization Society we learn that
from 1820 to 1833 only 2,885 Negroes were sent
to Africa by the Society. Furthermore, more
than 2,700 of this number were taken from the
slave States, and about two thirds of these were
slaves manumitted on the condition that they
would emigrate.[9] Later statistics show the
same tendency. By 1852, 7,836 had been de-

[8] *The Journal of Negro History*, I, pp. 284–296; Garrison,
Thoughts on Colonization, p. 204.

[9] *The African Repository*, XXXIII, p. 117.

ported from the United States to Liberia. 2,720
of these were born free, 204 purchased their
freedom, 3,868 were emancipated in view of
their going to Liberia and 1,044 were liberated
Africans returned by the United States Government.[10] Considering the fact that there were
434,495 free persons of color in this country in
1850 and 488,070 in 1860, the colonizationists
saw that the very element of the population
which the movement was intended to send out
of the country had increased rather than decreased. It is clear, then, that the American
Colonization Society, though regarded as a factor to play an important part in promoting the
exodus of the free Negroes to foreign soil, was
an inglorious failure.

Colonization in other quarters, however, was
not abandoned. A colony of Negroes in Texas
was contemplated in 1833 prior to the time when
the republic became independent of Mexico, as
slavery was not at first assured in that State.
The *New York Commercial Advertiser* had no
objection to the enterprise but felt that there
were natural obstacles such as a more expensive
conveyance than that to Monrovia, the high
price of land in that country, the Catholic religion to which Negroes were not accustomed to
conform, and their lack of knowledge of the
Spanish language. The editor observed that
some who had emigrated to Hayti a few years

[10] *The African Repository*, XXIII, p. 117.

before became discontented because they did not
know the language. Louisiana, a slave State,
moreover, would not suffer near its borders a
free Negro republic to serve as an asylum for
refugees.[11] The *Richmond Whig* saw the actual
situation in dubbing the scheme as chimerical
for the reason that a more unsuitable country
for the blacks did not exist. Socially and politically it would never suit the Negroes. Already
a great number of adventurers from the United
States had gone to Texas and fugitives from
justice from Mexico, a fierce, lawless and tur-
bulent class, would give the Negroes little
chance there, as the Negroes could not contend
with the Spaniard and the Creole. The editor
believed that an inferior race could never exist
in safety surrounded by a superior one despis-
ing them. Colonization in Africa was then
urged and the efforts of the blacks to go elsewhere were characterized as doing mischief at
every turn to defeat the ''enlightened plan'' for
the amelioration of the Negroes.[12]

It was still thought possible to induce the Negroes to go to some congenial foreign land, although few of them would agree to emigrate to
Africa. Not a few Negroes began during the
two decades immediately preceding the Civil
War to think more favorably of African colonization and a still larger number, in view of

[11] *The African Repository,* IX, pp. 86–88.
[12] *Ibid.,* IX, p. 88.

the increasing disabilities fixed upon their class, thought of migrating to some country nearer to the United States. Much was said about Central America, but British Guiana and the West Indies proved to be the most inviting fields to the latter-day Negro colonizationists. This idea was by no means new, for Jefferson in his foresight had, in a letter to Governor Edward Coles, of Illinois, in 1814, shown the possibilities of colonization in the West Indies. He felt that because Santo Domingo had become an independent Negro republic it would offer a solution of the problem as to where the Negroes should be colonized. In this way these islands would become a sort of safety valve for the United States. He became more and more convinced that all the West Indies would remain in the hands of the people of color, and a total expulsion of the whites sooner or later would take place. It was high time, he thought, that Americans should foresee the bloody scenes which their children certainly, and possibly they themselves, would have to wade through.[13]

[13] "If something is not done, and soon done," said he, "we shall be the murderers of our own children. The '*murmura venturos nautis prudentia ventos*' has already reached us (from Santo Domingo); the revolutionary storm, now sweeping the globe will be upon us, and happy if we make timely provision to give it an easy passage over our land. From the present state of things in Europe and America, the day which begins our combustion must be near at hand; and only a single spark is wanting to make that day to-morrow. If we had begun sooner, we might probably have been allowed a lengthier opera-

The movement to the West Indies was accelerated by other factors. After the emancipation in those islands in the thirties, there had for some years been a dearth of labor. Desiring to enjoy their freedom and living in a climate where there was not much struggle for life, the freedmen either refused to work regularly or wandered about purposely from year to year. The islands in which sugar had once played a conspicuous part as the foundation of their industry declined and something had to be done to meet this exigency. In the forties and fifties, therefore, there came to the United States a number of labor agents whose aim was to set forth the inviting aspect of the situation in the West Indies so as to induce free Negroes to try their fortunes there. To this end meetings were held in Baltimore, Philadelphia, New York and

tion to clear ourselves, but every day's delay lessens the time we may take for emancipation.''

As to the mode of emancipation, he was satisfied that that must be a matter of compromise between the passions, the prejudices, and the real difficulties which would each have its weight in that operation. He believed that the first chapter of this history, which was begun in St. Domingo, and the next succeeding ones, would recount how all the whites were driven from all the other islands. This, he thought, would prepare their minds for a peaceable accommodation between justice and policy; and furnish an answer to the difficult question, as to where the colored emigrants should go. He urged that the country put some plan under way, and the sooner it did so the greater would be the hope that it might be permitted to proceed peaceably toward consummation.—See Ford edition of *Jefferson's Writings*, VI, p. 349, VII, pp. 167, 168.

Boston and even in some of the cities of the
South, where these agents appealed to the free
Negroes to emigrate.[14]
Thus before the American Colonization Society had got well on its way toward accomplish-
ing its purpose of deporting the Negroes to
Africa the West Indies and British Guiana
claimed the attention of free people of color in
offering there unusual opportunities. After the
consummation of British emancipation in those
islands in 1838, the English nation came to be
regarded by the Negroes of the United States
as the exclusive friend of the race. The Negro
press and church vied with each other in prais-
ing British emancipation as an act of philanthropy and pointed to the English dominions as
an asylum for the oppressed. So disturbed
were the whites by this growing feeling that
riots broke out in northern cities on occasions of
Negro celebrations of the anniversary of emancipation in the West Indies.[15]
In view of these facts, the colonizationists had
to redouble their efforts to defend their cause.
They found it a little difficult to make a good
case for Liberia, a land far away in an un-
healthy climate so much unlike that of the West
Indies and British Guiana, where Negroes had

[14] *Letter of Mr. Stanbury Boyce;* and *The African Repository.*

[15] *Philadelphia Gazette,* Aug. 2, 3, 4, 8, 1842; *United States
Gazette,* Aug. 2–5, 1842; and the *Pennsylvanian,* Aug. 2, 3, 4,
8, 1842.

been declared citizens entitled to all privileges afforded by the government. The colonizationists could do no more than to express doubt that the Negroes would have there the opportunities for mental, moral and social betterment which were offered in Liberia. The promoters of the enterprise in Africa did not believe that the West Indian planters who had had emancipation forced upon them would accept blacks from the United States as their equals, nor that they, far from receiving the consideration of freedmen, would be there any more than menials. When told of the establishment of schools and churches for the improvemnt of the freedmen, the colonizationists replied that schools might be provided, but the planters could have no interest in encouraging education as they did not want an elevated class of people but bone and muscle. As an evidence of the truth of this statement it was asserted that newspapers of the country were filled with disastrous accounts of the falling off of crops and the scarcity of labor but had little to say about those forces instrumental in the uplift of the people.[16]

An effort was made also to show that there would be no economic advantage in going to the British dominions. It was thought that as soon as the first demand for labor was supplied wages would be reduced, for no new plantations could be opened there as in a growing country

[16] *The African Repository,* XVI, pp. 113–115.

like Liberia. It would be impossible, therefore, for the Negroes immigrating there to take up land and develop a class of small farmers as they were doing in Africa. Under such circumstances, they contended, the Negroes in the West Indies could not feel any of the "elevating influences of nationality of character," as the white men would limit the influence of the Negroes by retaining practically all of the wealth of the islands. The inducements, therefore, offered the free Negroes in the United States were merely intended to use them in supplying in the British dominions the need of men to do drudgery scarcely more elevating than the toil of slaves.[17]

Determined to interest a larger number of persons in diverting the attention of the free Negroes from the West Indies, the colonizationists took higher ground. They asserted that the interests of the millions of white men in this country were then at stake, and even if it would be better for the three million Negroes of the country gradually to emigrate to the British dominions, it would eventually prove prejudicial to the interests of the United States. They showed how the Negroes immigrating into the West Indies would be made to believe that the refusal to extend to them here social and political equality was cruel oppression and the immigrants, therefore, would carry with them no good will

17 *The African Repository,* XXI, p. 114.

to this country. When they arrived in the West
Indies their circumstances would increase this
hostility, alienate their affections and estrange
them wholly from the United States. Taught
to regard the British as the exclusive friends of
their race, devoted to its elevation, they would
become British in spirit. As such, these Negroes would be controlled by British influence
and would increase the wealth and commerce of
the British and as soldiers would greatly
strengthen British power.[18]

It was better, therefore, they argued, to direct
the Negroes to Liberia, for those who went there
with a feeling of hostility against the white people were placed in circumstances operating to
remove that feeling, in that the kind solicitude
for their welfare would be extended them in
their new home so as to overcome their prejudices, win their confidence, and secure their attachment. Looking to this country as their
fatherland and the home of their benefactors,
the Liberians would develop a nation, taking the
religion, customs and laws of this country as
their models, marketing their produce in this
country and purchasing our manufactures. In
spite of its independence, therefore, Liberia
would be American in feeling, language and interests, affording a means to get rid of a class
undesirable here but desirable to us there in

[18] *The African Repository*, XVI, p. 116.

their power to extend American influence, trade and commerce.[19]

Negroes migrated to the West Indies in spite of this warning and protest. Hayti, at first looked upon with fear of having a free Negro government near slaveholding States, became fixed in the minds of some as a desirable place for the colonization of free persons of color.[20] This was due to the apparent natural advantages in soil, climate and the situation of the country over other places in consideration. It was thought that the island would support fourteen millions of people and that, once opened to immigration from the United States, it would in a few years fill up by natural increase. It was remembered that it was formerly the emporium of the Western World and that it supplied both hemispheres with sugar and coffee. It had rapidly recovered from the disaster of the French Revolution and lacked only capital and education which the United States under these circumstances could furnish. Furthermore, it was argued that something in this direction should be immediately done, as European nations then seeking to establish friendly relations with the islands, would secure there commercial advantages which the United States should have and could establish by sending to that island free Negroes especially devoted to agriculture.

[19] *The African Repository*, XVI, p. 115.
[20] *Ibid.*, XVI, p. 116.

In 1836, Z. Kingsley, a Florida planter,[21] actually undertook to carry out such a plan on a

[21] Speaking of this colony Kingsley said: ''About eighteen months ago, I carried my son George Kingsley, a healthy colored man of uncorrupted morals, about thirty years of age, tolerably well educated, of very industrious habits, and a native of Florida, together with six prime African men, my own slaves, liberated for that express purpose, to the northeast side of the Island of Hayti, near Porte Plate, where we arrived in the month of October, 1836, and after application to the local authorities, from whom I rented some good land near the sea, and thickly timbered with lofty woods, I set them to work cutting down trees, about the middle of November, and returned to my home in Florida. My son wrote to us frequently, giving an account of his progress. Some of the fallen timber was dry enough to burn in January, 1837, when it was cleared up, and eight acres of corn planted, and as soon as circumstances would allow, sweet potatoes, yams, cassava, rice, beans, peas, plantains, oranges, and all sorts of fruit trees, were planted in succession. In the month of October, 1837, I again set off for Hayti, in a coppered brig of 150 tons, bought for the purpose and in five days and a half, from St. Mary's in Georgia, landed my son's wife and children, at Porte Plate, together with the wives and children of his servants, now working for him under an indenture of nine years; also two additional families of my slaves, all liberated for the express purpose of transportation to Hayti, where they were all to have as much good land in fee, as they could cultivate, say ten acres for each family, and all its proceeds, together with one-fourth part of the net proceeds of their labor, on my son's farm, for themselves; also victuals, clothes, medical attendance, etc., gratis, besides Saturdays and Sundays, as days of labor for themselves, or of rest, just at their option.''

''On my arrival at my son's place, called Cabaret (twenty-seven miles east of Porte Plate) in November, 1837, as before stated, I found everything in the most flattering and prosperous condition. They had all enjoyed good health, were overflowing with the most delicious variety and abundance of fruits and provisions, and were overjoyed at again meeting their wives small scale. He established on the northeast side of Hayti, near Port Plate, his son, George and children; whom they could introduce into good comfortable log houses, all nicely whitewashed, and in the midst of a profuse abundance of good provisions, as they had generally cleared five or six acres of their land each, which being very rich, and planted with every variety to eat or to sell on their own account, and had already laid up thitry or forty dollars apiece. My son's farm was upon a larger scale, and furnished with more commodious dwelling houses, also with store and out houses. In nine months he had made and housed three crops of corn, of twenty-five bushels to the acre, each, or one crop every three months. His highland rice, which was equal to any in Carolina, so ripe and heavy as some of it to be couched or leaned down, and no bird had ever troubled it, nor had any of his fields ever been hoed, or required hoeing, there being as yet no appearance of grass. His cotton was of an excellent staple. In seven months it had attained the height of thirteen feet; the stalks were ten inches in circumference, and had upwards of five hundred large boles on each stalk (not a worm nor red bug as yet to be seen). His yams, cassava, and sweet potatoes, were incredibly large, and plentifully thick in the ground; one kind of sweet potato, lately introduced from Taheita (formerly Otaheita) Island in the Pacific, was of peculiar excellence; tasted like new flour and grew to an ordinary size in one month. Those I ate at my son's place had been planted five weeks, and were as big as our full grown Florida potatoes. His sweet orange trees budded upon wild stalks cut off (which every where abound), about six months before had large tops, and the buds were swelling as if preparing to flower. My son reported that his people had all enjoyed good health and had labored just as steadily as they formerly did in Florida and were well satisfied with their situation and the advantageous exchange of circumstances they had made. They all enjoyed the friendship of the neighboring inhabitants and the entire confidence of the Haytian Government.''

''I remained with my son all January, 1838 and assisted him in making improvements of different kinds, amongst which was a new two-story house, and then left him to go to Port au

Kingsley, a well-educated colored man of industrious habits and uncorrupted morals, together with six "prime African men," slaves liberated for that express purpose. There he purchased for them 35,000 acres of land upon which they engaged in the production of crops indigenous to that soil.

Hayti, however, was not to be the only island to get consideration. In 1834 two hundred colored emigrants went from New York alone to Trinidad, under the superintendence and at the expense of planters of that island. It was later reported that every one of them found employment on the day of arrival and in one or two instances the most intelligent were placed as overseers at the salary of $500 per annum. No one received less than $1.00 a day and most of them earned $1.50. The Trinidad press welcomed these immigrants and spoke in the highest terms of the valuable services they rendered the country.[22] Others followed from year to year. One of these Negroes appreciated so much this new field of opportunity that he returned and in-

Prince, where I obtained a favorable answer from the President of Hayti, to his petition, asking for leave to hold in fee simple, the same tract of land upon which he then lived as a tenant, paying rent to the Haytian Government, containing about thirty-five thousand acres, which was ordered to be surveyed to him, and valued, and not expected to exceed the sum of three thousand dollars, or about ten cents an acre. After obtaining this land in fee for my son, I returned to Florida in February, in 1838.''—See *The African Repository*, XIV, pp. 215-216.

[22] *Niles Register*, LXVI, pp. 165, 386.

duced twenty intelligent free persons of color living in Annapolis, Maryland, also to emigrate to Trinidad.[23]

The New York Sun reported in 1840 that 160 colored persons left Philadelphia for Trinidad. They had been hired by an eminent planter to labor on that island and they were encouraged to expect that they should have privileges which would make their residence desirable. The editor wished a few dozen Trinidad planters would come to that city on the same business and on a much larger scale.[24] N. W. Pollard, agent of the Government of Trinidad, came to Baltimore in 1851 to make his appeal for emigrants, offering to pay all expenses.[25] At a meeting held in Baltimore, in 1852, the parents of Mr. Stanbury Boyce, now a retired merchant in Washington, District of Columbia, were also induced to go. They found there opportunities which they had never had before and well established themselves in their new home. The account which Mr. Boyce gives in a letter to the writer corroborates the newspaper reports as to the success of the enterprise.[26]

The New York Journal of Commerce reported in 1841 that, according to advices received at New Orleans from Jamaica, there had arrived in that island fourteen Negro emigrants from

23 *Niles Register*, LXVII, p. 180.
24 *The African Repository*, XVI, p. 28.
25 *Ibid.*, p. 29.
26 *Letter of Mr. Stanbury Boyce.*

the United States, being the first fruits of Mr. Barclay's mission to this country. A much larger number of Negroes were expected and various applications for their services had been received from respectable parties.[27] The products of soil were reported as much reduced from former years and to meet its demand for labor some freedmen from Sierra Leone were induced to emigrate to that island in 1842.[28] One Mr. Anderson, an agent of the government of Jamaica, contemplated visiting New York in 1851 to secure a number of laborers, tradesmen and agricultural settlers.[29]

In the course of time, emigration to foreign lands interested a larger number of representative Negroes. At a national council called in 1853 to promote more effectively the amelioration of the colored people, the question of emigration and that only was taken up for serious consideration. But those who desired to introduce the question of Liberian colonization or who were especially interested in that scheme were not invited. Among the persons who promoted the calling of this council were William Webb, Martin R. Delaney, J. Gould Bias, Franklin Turner, Augustus Greene, James M. Whitfield, William Lambert, Henry Bibb, James T. Holly and Henry M. Collins.

[27] St. Lucia and Trinidad were then considered unfavorable to the working of the new system.—See *The African Repository*, XXVII, p. 196.

[28] *Niles Register*, LXIII, p. 65.

[29] *Ibid.*, LXIII, p. 65.

There developed in this assembly three groups, one believing with Martin R. Delaney that it was best to go to the Niger Valley in Africa, another following the counsel of James M. Whitfield then interested in emigration to Central America, and a third supporting James T. Holly who insisted that Hayti offered the best opportunities for free persons of color desiring to leave the United States. Delaney was commissioned to proceed to Africa, where he succeeded in concluding treaties with eight African kings who offered American Negroes inducements to settle in their respective countries. James Redpath, already interested in the scheme of colonization in Hayti, had preceded Holly there and with the latter as his coworker succeeded in sending to that country as many as two thousand emigrants, the first of whom sailed from this country in 1861.[30] Owing to the lack of equipment adequate to the establishment of the settlement and the unfavorable climate, not more than one third of the emigrants remained. Some attention was directed to California and Central America just as in the case of Africa but nothing in that direction took tangible form immediately, and the Civil War following soon thereafter did not give some of these schemes a chance to materialize.

[30] Cromwell, *The Negro in American History*, pp. 43–44.

CHAPTER V

THE reader will naturally be interested in learning exactly what these thousands of Negroes did on free soil. To estimate these achievements the casual reader of contemporary testimony would now, as such persons did then, find it decidedly easy. He would say that in spite of the unfailing aid which philanthropists gave the blacks, they seldom kept themselves above want and, therefore, became a public charge, afflicting their communities with so much poverty, disease and crime that they were considered the lepers of society. The student of history, however, must look beyond these comments for the whole truth. One must take into consideration the fact that in most cases these Negroes escaped as fugitives without sufficient food and clothing to comfort them until they could reach free soil, lacking the small fund with which the pioneer usually provided himself in going to establish a home in the wilderness, and lacking, above all, initiative of which slavery had deprived them. Furthermore, these refugees with few exceptions had to go to places where they were not wanted and in some cases to points from which they were driven as unde-

sira'bles, although preparation for their coming
had sometimes gone to the extent of purchasing
homes and making provision for employment
upon arrival.[1] Several well-established Negro
settlements in the North, moreover, were broken
up by the slave hunters after the passing of the
Fugitive Slave Law of 1850.[2]
The increasing intensity of the hatred of the
Negroes must be understood too both as a cause
and result of their intolerable condition. Prior
to 1800 the Negroes of the North were in fair
circumstances. Until that time it was generally
believed that the whites and the blacks would
soon reach the advanced stage of living together
on a basis of absolute equality.[3] The Negroes
had not at that time exceeded the number that
could be assimilated by the sympathizing communities in that section. The intolerable legislation of the South, however, forced so many
free Negroes in the rough to crowd northern
cities during the first four decades of the nineteenth century that they could not be easily readjusted. The number seeking employment far
exceeded the demand for labor and thus multiplied the number of vagrants and paupers, many
of whom had already been forced to this condition by the Irish and Germans then immigrating
into northern cities. At one time, as in the case

---

[1] *Cincinnati Morning Herald*, July 17, 1846.

[2] Woodson, *The Education of the Negro Prior to 1861*, p. 242.

[3] Turner, *The Negro in Pennsylvania*, p. 143; *Correspondence
of Dr. Benjamin Rush*, XXXIX, p. 41.

of Philadelphia, the Negroes constituting a small fraction of the population furnished one half of the criminals.[4] A radical opposition to the Negro followed, therefore, arousing first the laboring classes and finally alienating the support of the well-to-do people and the press. This condition obtained until 1840 in most northern communities and until 1850 in some places where the Negro population was considerable. We must also take into account the critical labor situation during these years. The northern people were divided as to the way the Negroes should be encouraged. The mechanics of the North raised no objection to having the Negroes freed and enlightened but did not welcome them to that section as competitors in the struggle of life. When, therefore, the blacks, converted to the doctrine of training the hand to work with skill, began to appear in northern industrial centers there arose a formidable prejudice against them.[5] Negro and white mechanics had once worked together but during the second quarter of the nineteenth century, when labor became more dignified and a larger number of white persons devoted themselves to skilled labor, they adopted the policy of eliminating the blacks. This opposition, to be sure,

---

[4] DuBois, *The Philadelphia Negro*, pp. 26–27.

[5] *The Journal of Negro History*, I, p. 5; and *Proceedings of the American Convention of Abolition Societies*.

was not a mere harmless sentiment. It tended to give rise to the organization of labor groups and finally to that of trades unions, the beginnings of those controlling this country to-day. Carrying the fight against the Negro still further, these laboring classes used their influence to obtain legislation against the employment of Negroes in certain pursuits. Maryland and Georgia passed laws restricting the privileges of Negro mechanics, and Pennsylvania followed their example.[6]

Even in those cases when the Negroes were not disturbed in their new homes on free soil, it was, with the exception of the Quaker and a few other communities, merely an act of toleration.[7] It must not be concluded, however, that the Negroes then migrating to the North did not receive considerable aid. The fact to be noted here is that because they were not well received sometimes by the people of their new environment, the help which they obtained from friends afar off did not suffice to make up for the deficiency of community cooperation. This, of course, was an unusual handicap to the Negro, as his life as a slave tended to make him a dependent rather than a pioneer.

It is evident, however, from accessible statistics that wherever the Negro was adequately encouraged he succeeded. When the urban Ne-

[6] DuBois and Dill, *The Negro American Artisan*, p. 36.
[7] Jay, *An Inquiry*, pp. 34, 108, 109, 114.

groes in northern communities had emerged
from their crude state they easily learned from
the white men their method of solving the problems of life. This tendency was apparent after
1840 and striking results of their efforts were
noted long before the Civil War. They showed
an inclination to work when positions could be
found, purchased homes, acquired other property, built churches and established schools.
Going even further than this, some of them, taking advantage of their opportunities in the business world, accumulated considerable fortunes,
just as had been done in certain centers in the
South where Negroes had been given a chance.[8]

In cities far north like Boston not so much difference as to the result of this migration was
noted. Some economic progress among the Negroes had early been observed there as a result
of the long residence of Negroes in that city as
in the case of Lewis Hayden who established a
successful clothing business.[9] In New York
such evidences were more apparent. There
were in that city not so many Negroes as fre-
quented some other northern communities of
this time but enough to make for that city a decidedly perplexing problem. It was the usual
situation of ignorant, helpless fugitives and free
Negroes going, they knew not where, to find a
better country. The situation at times became

[8] *The Journal of Negro History*, I, pp. 20–22.
[9] Delany, *Condition of the Colored People*, p. 106.

so grave that it not only caused prejudice but gave rise to intense opposition against those who defended the cause of the blacks as in the case of the abolition riots which occurred at several places in the State in 1834.[10] To relieve this situation, Gerrit Smith, an unusually philanthropic gentleman, came forward with an interesting plan. Having large tracts of land in the southeastern counties of New York, he proposed to settle on small farms a large number of those Negroes huddled together in the congested districts of New York City. Desiring to obtain only the best class, he requested that the Negroes to be thus colonized be recommended by Reverend Charles B. Ray, Reverend Theodore S. Wright and Dr. J. McCune Smith, three Negroes of New York City, known to be representative of the best of the race. Upon their recommendations he deeded unconditionally to black men in 1846 three hundred small farms in Franklin, Essex, Hamilton, Fulton, Oneida, Delaware, Madison and Ulster counties, giving to each settler beside $10.00 to enable him to visit his farm.[11] With these holdings the blacks would not only have a basis for economic independence but would have sufficient property to meet the special qualifications which New York by the law of 1823 required of Negroes offering to vote.

[10] *The Liberator,* July 9, 1835.
[11] Hammond, *Gerrit Smith,* pp. 26–27.

This experiment, however, was a failure. It was not successful because of the intractability of the land, the harshness of the climate, and, in a great measure, the inefficiency of the settlers. They had none of the qualities of farmers. Furthermore, having been disabled by infirmities and vices they could not as beneficiaries answer the call of the benefactor. Peterboro, the town opened to Negroes in this section, did maintain a school and served as a station of the Underground Railroad but the agricultural results expected of the enterprise never materialized. The main difficulty in this case was the impossibility of substituting something foreign for individual enterprise.[12]

Progressive Negroes did appear, however, in other parts of the State. In Penyan, Western New York, William Platt and Joseph C. Cassey were successful lumber merchants.[13] Mr. W. H. Topp of Albany was for several years one of the leading merchant tailors of that city.[14] Henry Scott, of New York City, developed a successful pickling business, supplying most of the vessels entering that port.[15] Thomas Downing for thirty years ran a creditable restaurant in the midst of the Wall Street banks, where he made a fortune.[16] Edward V. Clark conducted

[12] *Frothingham, Gerrit Smith,* p. 73.
[13] Delany, *Condition of the Colored People,* pp. 107–108.
[14] *Ibid.,* p. 102.
[15] *Ibid.,* p. 102.
[16] *Ibid.,* pp. 103–104.

a thriving business, handling jewelry and silverware.[17] The Negroes as a whole, moreover, had shown progress. Aided by the Government and philanthropic white people, they had before the Civil War a school system with primary, intermediate and grammar schools and a normal department. They then had considerable property, several churches and some benevolent institutions.

In Southern Pennsylvania, nearer to the border between the slave and free States, the effects of the achievements of these Negroes were more apparent for the reason that in these urban centers there were sufficient Negroes for one to be helpful to the other. Philadelphia presented then the most striking example of the remaking of these people. Here the handicap of the foreign element was greatest, especially after 1830. The Philadelphia Negro, moreover, was further impeded in his progress by the presence of southerners who made Philadelphia their home, and still more by the prejudice of those Philadelphia merchants who, sustaining such close relations to the South, hated the Negro and the abolitionists who antagonized their customers.

In spite of these untoward circumstances, however, the Negroes of Philadelphia achieved success. Negroes who had formerly been able to toil upward were still restricted but they had

[17] Delany, *Condition of the Colored People*, pp. 106–107.

learned to make opportunities. In 1832 the Philadelphia blacks had $350,000 of taxable property, $359,626 in 1837 and $400,000 in 1847. These Negroes had 16 churches and 100 benevolent societies in 1837 and 19 churches and 106 benevolent societies in 1847. Philadelphia then had more successful Negro schools than any other city in the country. There were also about 500 Negro mechanics in spite of the opposition of organized labor.[18] Some of these Negroes, of course, were natives of that city. Chief among those who had accumulated considerable property was Mr. James Forten, the proprietor of one of the leading sail manufactories, constantly employing a large number of men, black and white. Joseph Casey, a broker of considerable acumen, also accumulated desirable property, worth probably $75,000.[19] Crowded out of the higher pursuits of labor, certain other enterprising business men of this group organized the Guild of Caterers. This was composed of such men as Bogle, Prosser, Dorsey, Jones and Minton. The aim was to elevate the Negro waiter and cook from the plane of menials to that of progressive business men. Then came Stephen Smith who amassed a large fortune as a lumber merchant and with him Whipper, Vidal and Purnell. Still and Bowers were

[18] DuBois, *The Philadelphia Negro*, p. 31; *Report of the Condition of the Free People of Color*, 1838; *ibid.*, 1849; and Bacon, *Statistics of the Colored People of Philadelphia*, 1859.
[19] Delany, *Condition of the Colored People*, p. 95.

reliable coal merchants, Adger a success in handling furniture, Bowser a well-known painter, and William H. Riley the intelligent boot-maker.[20] There were a few such successful Negroes in other communities in the State. Mr. William Goodrich, of York, acquired considerable interest in the branch of the Baltimore and Ohio Railroad extending to Lancaster.[21] Benjamin Richards, of Pittsburgh, amassed a large fortune running a butchering business, buying by contract droves of cattle to supply the various military posts of the United States.[22] Mr. Henry M. Collins, who started life as a boatman, left this position for speculation in real estate in Pittsburgh where he established himself as an asset of the community and accumulated considerable wealth.[23] Owen A. Barrett, of the same city, made his way by discovering the remedy known as *B. A. Fahnestock's Celebrated Vermifuge,* for which he was retained in the employ of the proprietor, who exploited the remedy.[24] Mr. John Julius made himself indispensable to Pittsburgh by running the Concert Hall Cafe where he served President William Henry Harrison in 1840.[25]

20 DuBois, *The Philadelphia Negro*, pp. 31–36.
21 Delany, *Condition of the Colored People*, p. 109.
22 *Ibid.*, p. 101.
23 *Ibid.*, p. 104.
24 *Ibid.*, p. 105.
25 *Ibid.*, p. 107.

The field of greatest achievement, however, was not in the conservative East where the people had well established their going toward an enlightened and sympathetic aristocracy of talent and wealth. It was in the West where men were in position to establish themselves anew and make of life what they would. These crude communities, to be sure, often objected to the presence of the Negroes and sometimes drove them out. But, on the other hand, not a few of those centers in the making were in the hands of the Quakers and other philanthropic persons who gave the Negroes a chance to grow up with the community, when they exhibited a capacity which justified philanthropic efforts in their behalf.

These favorable conditions obtained especially in the towns along the Ohio river, where so many fugitives and free persons of color stopped on their way from slavery to freedom. In Steubenville a number of Negroes had by their industry and good deportment made themselves helpful to the community. Stephen Mulber who had been in that town for thirty years was in 1835 the leader of a group of thrifty free persons of color. He had a brick dwelling, in which he lived, and other property in the city. He made his living as a master mechanic employing a force of workmen to meet the increasing demand for his labor.[26] In Gallipolis,

---

[26] *The Journal of Negro History,* I, p. 22.

there was another group of this class of Negroes, who had permanently attached themselves to the town by the acquisition of property. They were then able not only to provide for their families but were maintaining also a school and a church.[27] In Portsmouth, Ohio, despite the ''Black Friday'' upheaval of 1831, the Negroes settled down to the solution of the problems of their new environment and later showed in the accumulation of property evidences of actual progress. Among the successful Negroes in Columbus was David Jenkins who acquired considerable property as a painter, glazier and paper hanger.[28] One Mr. Hill, of Chillicothe, was for several years its leading tanner and currier.[29]

It was in Cincinnati, however, that the Negroes made most progress in the West. The migratory blacks came there at times in such large numbers, as we have observed, that they provoked the hostile classes of whites to employ rash measures to exterminate them. But the Negroes, accustomed to adversity, struggled on, endeavoring through schools and churches to embrace every opportunity to rise. By 1840 there were 2,255 Negroes in that city. They had, exclusive of personal effects and $19,000 worth of church property, accumulated $209,000

[27] Hickok, *The Negro in Ohio*, p. 88.
[28] Delany, *Condition of the Colored People*, p. 99.
[29] *Ibid.*, p. 101.

worth of real estate. A number of their progressive men had established a real estate firm known as the "Iron Chest" company which built houses for Negroes. One man, who had once thought it unwise to accumulate wealth from which he might be driven, had, by 1840, changed his mind and purchased $6,000 worth of real estate.

Another Negro paid $5,000 for himself and family and bought a home worth $800 or $1,000. A freedman, who was a slave until he was twenty-four years of age, then had two lots worth $10,000, paid a tax of $40 and had 320 acres of land in Mercer County. Another, who was worth only $3,000 in 1836, had seven houses in 1840, 400 acres of land in Indiana, and another tract in Mercer County, Ohio. He was worth altogether about $12,000 or $15,000. A woman who was a slave until she was thirty was then worth $2,000. She had also come into potential possession of two houses on which a white lawyer had given her a mortgage to secure the payment of $2,000 borrowed from this thrifty woman. Another Negro, who was on the auction block in 1832, had spent $2,600 purchasing himself and family and had bought two brick houses worth $6,000 and 560 acres of land in Mercer County, Ohio, said to be worth $2,500.[30]

[30] *The Philanthropist,* July 21, 1840, gives these statistics in detail.

The Negroes of Cincinnati had as early as 1820 established schools which developed during the forties into something like a modern system with Gilmore's High School as a capstone. By that time they had also not only several churches but had given time and means to the organization and promotion of such as the *Sabbath School Youth's Society*, the *Total Abstinence Temperance Society* and the *Anti-Slavery Society*. The worthy example set by the Negroes of this city was a stimulus to noble endeavor and significant achievements of Negroes throughout the Ohio and Mississippi Valleys. Disarming their enemies of the weapon that they would continue a public charge, they secured the cooperation of a larger number of white people who at first had treated them with contempt.[31]

This unusual progress in the Ohio valley had been promoted by two forces, the development of the steamboat as a factor in transportation and the rise of the Negro mechanic. Negroes employed on vessels as servants to the travelling public amassed large sums received in the form of tips. Furthermore, the fortunate few, constituting the stewards of these vessels, could by placing contracts for supplies and using business methods realize handsome incomes. Many Negroes thus enriched purchased real estate and went into business in towns along the Ohio.

[31] *The Philanthropist*, July 21, 1840.

The other force, the rise of the Negro mechanic, was made possible by overcoming much of the prejudice which had at first been encountered. A great change in this respect had taken place in Cincinnati by 1840.[32] Many Negroes who had been forced to work as menial laborers then had the opportunity to show their usefulness to their families and to the community. Negro mechanics were then getting as much skilled labor as they could do. It was not uncommon for white artisans to solicit employment of colored men because they had the reputation of being better paymasters than master workmen of the favored race. White mechanics not only worked with the blacks but often associated with them, patronized the same barber shop, and went to the same places of amusement.[33]

Out of this group came some very useful Negroes, among whom may be mentioned Robert Harlan, the horseman; A. V. Thompson, the tailor; J. Presley and Thomas Ball, contractors, and Samuel T. Wilcox, the merchant, who was worth $60,000 in 1859.[34] There were among them two other successful Negroes, Henry Boyd and Robert Gordon. Boyd was a Kentucky freedman who helped to overcome the prejudice in Cincinnati against Negro mechanics by inventing and exploiting a corded bed, the demand

[32] *The Cincinnati Daily Gazette,* Sept. 14, 1841.
[33] Barber's *Report on Colored People in Ohio.*
[34] Delany, *Condition of the Colored People,* pp. 97, 98.

for which was extensive throughout the Ohio and Mississippi valleys. He had a creditable manufacturing business in which he employed twenty-five men.[35] Robert Gordon was a much more interesting man. He was born a slave in Richmond, Virginia. He ingratiated himself into the favor of his master who placed him in charge of a large coal yard with the privilege of selling the slake for his own benefit. In the course of time, he accumulated in this position thousands of dollars with which he finally purchased himself and moved away to free soil. After observing the situation in several of the northern centers, he finally decided to settle in Cincinnati, where he arrived with $15,000. Knowing the coal business, he well established himself there after some discouragement and opposition. He accumulated much wealth which he invested in United States bonds during the Civil War and in real estate on Walnut Hills when the bonds were later redeemed.[36]

The ultimately favorable attitude of the people of Detroit toward immigrating Negroes had been reflected by the position the people of that section had taken from the time of the earliest settlements. Generally speaking, Detroit adhered to this position.[37] In this congenial com-

---

[35] Delany, *Condition of the Colored People*, p. 98.

[36] These facts were obtained from his children and from Cincinnati city directories.

[37] *Niles Register*, LXIX, p. 357.

munity prospered many a Negro family. There were the Williams' most of whom confined themselves to their trade of bricklaying and amassed considerable wealth. Then there were the Cooks, descending from Lomax B. Cook, a broker of no little business ability. Will Marion Cook, the musician, belongs to this family. The De Baptistes, too, were among the first to succeed in this new home, as they prospered materially from their experience and knowledge previously acquired in Fredericksburg, Virginia, as contractors. From this group came Richard De Baptiste, who in his day was the most useful Negro Baptist preacher in the Northwest.[38] The Pelhams were no less successful in establishing themselves in the economic world. Having an excellent reputation in the community, they easily secured the cooperation of the influential white people in the city. Out of this family came Robert A. Pelham, for years editor of a weekly in Detroit, and from 1901 to the present time an employee of the Federal Government in Washington.

The children of the Richards, another old family, were in no sense inferior to the descendants of the others. The most prominent and the most useful to emerge from this group was the daughter, Fannie M. Richards. She was born in Fredericksburg, Virginia, October 1, 1841. Having left that State with her parents

[38] Letters received from Miss Fannie M. Richards of Detroit.

when she was quite young, she did not see so much of the antebellum conditions obtaining there. Desiring to have better training than what was then given to persons of color in Detroit, she went to Toronto where she studied English, history, drawing and needlework. In later years she attended the Teachers' Training School in Detroit. She became a public-school teacher there in 1863 and after fifty years of creditable service in this work she was retired on a pension in 1913.[39]

The Negroes in the North had not only shown their ability to rise in the economic world when properly encouraged but had begun to exhibit power of all kinds. There were Negro inventors, a few lawyers, a number of physicians and dentists, many teachers, a score of intelligent preachers, some scholars of note, and even successful blacks in the finer arts. Some of these, with Frederick Douglass as the most influential, were also doing creditable work in journalism with about thirty newspapers which had developed among the Negroes as weapons of defense.[40]

This progress of the Negroes in the North was much more marked after the middle of the nineteenth century. The migration of Negroes to northern communities was at first checked by

[39] These facts were obtained from clippings taken from Detroit newspapers and from letters bearing on Miss Richard's career.

[40] *The A. M. E. Church Review*, IV, p. 309; and XX, p. 137.

the reaction in those places during the thirties and forties. Thus relieved of the large influx which once constituted a menace, those communities gave the Negroes already on hand better economic opportunities. It was fortunate too that prior to the check in the infiltration of the blacks they had come into certain districts in sufficiently large numbers to become a more potential factor.[41] They were strong enough in some cases to make common cause against foes and could by cooperation solve many problems with which the blacks in dispersed condition could not think of grappling.

Their endeavors along these lines proceeded in many cases from well-organized efforts like those culminating in the numerous national conventions which began meeting first in Philadelphia in 1830 and after some years of deliberation in this city extended to others in the North.[42] These bodies aimed not only to promote education, religion and morals, but, taking up the work which the Quakers began, they put forth efforts to secure to the free blacks opportunities to be trained in the mechanic arts to equip themselves for participation in the industries then springing up throughout the North. This movement, however, did not succeed in the proportion to the efforts put

[41] *Censuses of the United States;* and Clark, *Present Condition of Colored People.*

[42] *Minutes and Proceedings* of the Annual Convention of the People of Color.

forth because of the increasing power of the trades unions.

After the middle of the nineteenth century too the Negroes found conditions a little more favorable to their progress than the generation before. The aggressive South had by that time so shaped the policy of the nation as not only to force the free States to cease aiding the escape of fugitives but to undertake to impress the northerner into the service of assisting in their recapture as provided in the Fugitive Slave Law. This repressive measure set a larger number of the people thinking of the Negro as a national problem rather than a local one. The attitude of the North was then reflected in the personal liberty laws as an answer to this measure and in the increasing sympathy for the Negroes. During this decade, therefore, more was done in the North to secure to the Negroes better treatment and to give them opportunities for improvement.

CHAPTER VI

CONFUSING MOVEMENTS

THE Civil War waged largely in the South started the most exciting movement of the Negroes hitherto known. The invading Union forces drove the masters before them, leaving the slaves and sometimes poor whites to escape where they would or to remain in helpless condition to constitute a problem for the northern army.[1] Many poor whites of the border States went with the Confederacy, not always because they wanted to enter the war, but to choose what they considered the lesser of two evils. The slaves soon realized a community of interests with the Union forces sent, as they thought, to deliver them from thralldom. At first, it was difficult to determine a fixed policy for dealing with these fugitives. To drive them away was an easy matter, but this did not solve the problem. General Butler's action at Fortress Monroe in 1861, however, anticipated the policy finally adopted by the Union forces.[2] Hearing that three fugitive slaves who were received into

---

[1] This is well treated in John Eaton's *Grant, Lincoln and the Freedmen*. See also Coffin's *Boys of '61*.

[2] Williams, *History of the Negro Troops in the War of the Rebellion*, p. 70.

his lines were to have been employed in building fortifications for the Confederate army, he declared them seized as contraband of war rather than declare them actually free as did General Fremont[3] and General Hunter.[4] He then gave them employment for wages and rations and appropriated to the support of the unemployed a portion of the earnings of the laborers. This policy was followed by General Wood, Butler's successor, and by General Banks in New Orleans.

An elaborate plan for handling such fugitives was carried out by E. S. Pierce and General Rufus Saxton at Port Royal, South Carolina. Seeing the situation in another light, however, General Halleck in charge in the West excluded slaves from the Union lines, at first, as did General Dix in Virginia. But Halleck, in his instructions to General McCullum, February, 1862, ordered him to put contrabands to work to pay for food and clothing.[5] Other commanders, like General McCook and General Johnson, permitted the slave hunters to enter their lines and take their slaves upon identification,[6] ignoring the confiscation act of August, 1861, which was construed by some as justifying the retention of such refugees. Officers of a different attitude, however, soon began to pro-

---

[3] Greely, *American Conflict*, I, p. 585.

[4] *Ibid.*, II, p. 246.

[5] *Official Records of the Rebellion*, VIII, p. 628.

[6] Williams, *Negro Troops*, p. 66 et seq.

test against the returning of fugitive slaves. General Grant, also, while admitting the binding force of General Halleck's order, refused to grant permits to those in search of fugitives seeking asylum within his lines and at the capture of Fort Donelson ordered the retention of all blacks who had been used by the Confederates in building fortifications.[7]

Lincoln finally urged the necessity for withholding fugitive slaves from the enemy, believing that there could be in it no danger of servile insurrection and that the Confederacy would thereby be weakened.[8] As this opinion soon developed into a conviction that official action was necessary, Congress, by Act of March 13, 1862, provided that slaves be protected against the claims of their pursuers. Continuing further in this direction, the Federal Government gradually reached the position of withdrawing Negro labor from the Confederate territory. Finally the United States Government adopted the policy of withholding from the Confederates, slaves received with the understanding that their masters were in rebellion against the United States. With this as a settled policy then, the United States Government had to work out some scheme for the remaking of these fugitives coming into its camps.

In some of these cases the fugitives found

---

[7] *Official Records of the Rebellion*, VIII, p. 370; Williams, *Negro Troops*, p. 75.

[8] Eaton, *Grant, Lincoln and the Freedmen*, pp. 87, 92.

themselves among men more hostile to them
than their masters were, for many of the Union
soldiers of the border States were slaveholders
themselves and northern soldiers did not understand that they were fighting to free Negroes.
The condition in which they were on arriving,
moreover, was a new problem for the army.
Some came naked, some in decrepitude, some
afflicted with disease, and some wounded in their
efforts to escape.[9] There were "women in trav-
ail, the helplessness of childhood and of old
age, the horrors of sickness and of frequent
deaths."[10] In their crude state few of them had
any conception of the significance of liberty,
thinking that it meant idleness and freedom
from restraint. In consequence of this ignorance there developed such undesirable habits
as deceit, theft and licentiousness to aggravate
the afflictions of nakedness, famine and disease.[11]

In the East large numbers of these refugees
were concentrated at Washington, Alexandria,
Fortress Monroe, Hampton, Craney Island and
Fort Norfolk. There were smaller groups of
them at Yorktown, Suffolk and Portsmouth.[12]

[9] Pierce, *Freedmen of Port Royal, South Carolina*, passim;
Botume, *First Days Among the Contrabands*, pp. 10–22; and
Pearson, *Letters from Port Royal*, passim.
[10] Eaton, *Grant, Lincoln and the Freedmen*, p. 92.
[11] *Ibid.*, pp. 2, 3.
[12] Report of the *Committee of Representatives of the New
York Yearly Meeting of Friends* upon the *Condition and Wants
of the Colored Refugees*, 1862, p. 1 et seq.

Some of them were conducted from these camps into York, Columbia, Harrisburg, Pittsburgh and Philadelphia, and by water to New York and Boston, from which they went to various parts seeking labor. Some collected in groups as in the case of those at Five Points in New York.[13] Large numbers of them from Virginia assembled in Washington in 1862 in Duff Green's Row on Capitol Hill where they were organized as a camp, out of which came a contraband school, after being moved to the McClellan Barracks.[14] Then there was in the District of Columbia another group known as Freedmen's village on Arlington Heights. It was said that, in 1864, 30,000 to 40,000 Negroes had come from the plantations to the District of Columbia.[15] It happened here too as in most cases of this migration that the Negroes were on hand before the officials grappling with many other problems could determine exactly what could or should be done with them. The camps near Washington fortunately became centers for the employment of contrabands in the city. Those repairing to Fortress Monroe were distributed as laborers among the farmers of that vicinity.[16]

[13] *Report of the Committee of Representatives, etc.*, p. 3.

[14] At an entertainment of this school, Senator Pomeroy of Kansas, voicing the sentiment of Lincoln, spoke in favor of a scheme to colonize Negroes in Central America.

[15] *Special Report* of the United States Commission of Education on the Schools of the District of Columbia, p. 215.

[16] *Christian Examiner*, LXXVI, p. 349.

In some of these camps, and especially in those
of the West, the refugees were finally sent out
to other sections in need of labor, as in the cases
of the contrabands assembled with the Union
army at first at Grand Junction and later at
Memphis.[17]

There were three types of these camp communities which attracted attention as places for
free labor experimentation. These were at Port
Royal, on the Mississippi in the neighborhood of
Vicksburg, and in Lower Louisiana and Virginia. The first trial of free labor of blacks on
a large scale in a slave State was made in Port
Royal.[18] The experiment was generally successful. By industry, thrift and orderly conduct
the Negroes showed their appreciation for their
new opportunities. In the Mississippi section
invaded by the northern army, General Thomas
opened what he called *Infirmary Farms* which
he leased to Negroes on certain terms which
they usually met successfully. The same plan,
however, was not so successful in the Lower
Mississippi section.[19] The failure in this section was doubtless due to the inferior type of
blacks in the lower cotton belt where Negroes
had been more brutalized by slavery.

In some cases, these refugees experienced

[17] Eaton, *Lincoln, Grant and the Freedmen*, pp. 18, 30.
[18] Pierce, *The Freedmen of Port Royal, South Carolina, Official Reports;* and Pearson, *Letters from Port Royal written at
the Time of the Civil War.*
[19] *Christian Examiner*, LXXVI, p. 354.

many hardships. It was charged that they were worked hard, badly treated and deprived of all their wages except what was given them for rations and a scanty pittance, wholly insufficient to purchase necessary clothing and provide for their families.[20] Not a few of the refugees for these reasons applied for permission to return to their masters and sometimes such permission was granted; for, although under military authority, they were by order of Congress to be considered as freemen. These voluntary slaves, of course, were few and the authorities were not thereby impressed with the thought that Negroes would prefer to be slaves, should they be treated as freemen rather than as brutes.[21]

It became increasingly difficult, however, to handle this problem. In the first place, it was not an easy matter to find soldiers well disposed to serve the Negroes in any manner whatever and the officers of the army had no desire to force them to render such services since those thus engaged suffered a sort of social ostracism. The same condition obtained in the case of caring for those afflicted with disease, until there was issued a specific regulation placing the contraband sick in charge of the army surgeons.[22] What the situation in the Mississippi

[20] *Continental Monthly*, II, p. 193.

[21] *Report* of the Committee of Representatives of the New York Yearly Meeting of Friends, p. 12.

[22] Eaton, *Lincoln, Grant and the Freedmen*, p. 2.

Valley was during these months has been well described by an observer, saying: "I hope I may never be called on again to witness the horrible scenes I saw in those first days of history of the freedmen in the Mississippi Valley. Assistants were hard to find, especially the kind that would do any good in the camps. A detailed soldier in each camp of a thousand people was the best that could be done and his duties were so onerous that he ended by doing nothing. In reviewing the condition of the people at that time, I am not surprised at the marvelous stories told by visitors who caught an occasional glimpse of the misery and wretchedness in these camps. Our efforts to do anything for these people, as they herded together in masses, when founded on any expectation that they would help themselves, often failed; they had become so completely broken down in spirit, through suffering, that it was almost impossible to arouse them."[23]

A few sympathetic officers and especially the chaplains undertook to relieve the urgent cases of distress. They could do little, however, to handle all the problems of the unusual situation until they engaged the attention of the higher officers of the army and the federal functionaries in Washington. After some delay this was finally done and special officers were de-

[23] Eaton, *Lincoln, Grant and the Freedmen*, p. 19. See also Botume's *First Days Amongst the Contrabands*. This work vividly portrays conditions among the refugees assembled at points in South Carolina.

tailed to take charge of the contrabands. The Negroes were assembled in camps and employed according to instructions from the Secretary of War as teamsters, laborers and the like on forts and railroads. Some were put to picking, ginning, baling and removing cotton on plantations abandoned by their masters. General Grant, as early as 1862, was making further use of them as fatigue men in the department of the surgeon-general, the quartermaster and the commissary. He believed then that such Negroes as did well in these more humble positions should be made citizens and soldiers.[24] As a matter of fact out of this very suggestion came the policy of arming the Negroes, the first regiment of whom was recruited under orders issued by General Hunter at Port Royal, South Carolina in 1862. As the arming of the slave to participate in this war did not generally please the white people who considered the struggle a war between civilized groups, this policy could not offer general relief to the congested contraband camps.[25]

A better system of handling the fugitives was finally worked out, however, with a general superintendent at the head of each department, supported by a number of competent assistants. More explicit instructions were given as to the manner of dealing with the situation. It was to

[24] Eaton, *Grant, Lincoln and the Freedmen*, p. 15.
[25] Williams, *Negro in the Rebellion*, pp. 90–98.

be the duty of the superintendent of contrabands, says the order, to organize them into working parties in saving the cotton, as pioneers on railroads and steamboats, and in any way where their services could be made available. Where labor was performed for private individuals they were charged in accordance with the orders of the commander of the department. In case they were directed to save abandoned crops of cotton for the benefit of the United States Government, the officer selling such crops would turn over to the superintendent of contrabands the proceeds of the sale, which together with other earnings were used for clothing and feeding the Negroes. Clothing sent by philanthropic persons to these camps was received and distributed by the superintendent. In no case, however, were Negroes to be forced into the service of the United States Government or to be enticed away from their homes except when it became a military necessity.[26]

Some order out of the chaos eventually developed, for as John Eaton, one of the workers in the West, reported: "There was no promiscuous intermingling. Families were established by themselves. Every man took care of his own wife and children." "One of the most touching features of our Work," says he, "was

[26] *Official Records of the War of the Rebellion*, VII, pp. 503, 510, 560, 595, 628, 668, 698, 699, 711, 723, 739, 741, 757, 769, 787, 801, 802, 811, 818, 842, 923, 934; VIII, pp. 444, 445, 451, 464, 555, 556, 564, 584, 637, 642, 686, 690, 693, 825.

the eagerness with which colored men and women availed themselves of the opportunities offered them to legalize unions already formed, some of which had been in existence for a long time."[27] "Chaplain A. S. Fiske on one occasion married in about an hour one hundred and nineteen couples at one service, chiefly those who had long lived together." Letters from the Virginia camps and from those of Port Royal indicate that this favorable condition generally obtained.[28]

This unusual problem in spite of additional effort, however, would not readily admit of solution. Benevolent workers of the North, therefore, began to minister to the needs of these unfortunate blacks. They sent considerable sums of money, increasing quantities of clothing and even some of their most devoted men and women to toil among them as social workers and teachers.[29] These efforts also took organized form in various parts of the North under the direction of *The Pennsylvania Freedmen's Relief Association, The Tract Society, The American Missionary Association, Pennsylvania Friends Freedmen's Relief Association, Old School Presbyterian Mission, The Reformed Presbyterian Mission, The New England Freedmen's*

---

[27] Eaton, *Grant, Lincoln and the Freedmen*, pp. 34–35.

[28] Ames, *From a New England Woman's Diary*, passim; and Pearson, *Letters from Port Royal*, passim.

[29] Ames, *From a New England Woman's Diary in 1865*, passim.

Aid Committee, The New England Freedmen's Aid Society, The New England Freedmen's Mission, The Washington Christian Union, The Universalists of Maine, The New York Freedmen's Relief Association, The Hartford Relief Society, The National Freedmen's Relief Association of the District of Columbia, and finally the *Freedmen's Bureau.*[30]

As an outlet to the congested grouping of Negroes and poor whites in the war camps it was arranged to send a number of them to the loyal States as fast as there presented themselves opportunities for finding homes and employment. Cairo, Illinois, in the West, became the center of such activities extending its ramifications into all parts of the invaded southern territory. Some of the refugees permanently settled in the North, taking up the work abandoned by the northern soldiers who went to war.[31] It was soon found necessary to appoint a superintendent of such affairs at Cairo, for there were those who, desiring to lead a straggling life, had to be restrained from crime by military surveillance and regulations requiring labor for self-support. Exactly how many whites and blacks were thus aided to reach northern communities cannot be determined but in view of the frequent mention of their movements by travellers the number

[30] *Special Report* of the United States Commissioner of Education on the Schools of the District of Columbia, p. 217.

[31] Eaton, *Grant, Lincoln and the Freedmen*, p. 37.

must have been considerable. In some cases, as in Lawrence, Kansas, there were assembled enough freedmen to constitute a distinct group.[32] Speaking of this settlement the editor of the *Alton Telegraph* said in 1862 that although they amounted to many hundreds not one, that he could learn of, had been a public charge. They readily found employment at fair wages, and soon made themselves comfortable.[33]

There was a little apprehension that the North would be overrun by such blacks. Some had no such fear, however, for the reason that the census did not indicate such a movement. Many slaves were freed in the North prior to 1860, yet with all the emigration from the slave States to the North there were then in all the Northern States but 226,152 free blacks, while there were in the slave States 261,918, an excess of 35,766 in the slave States. Frederick Starr believed that during the Civil War there might be an influx for a few months but it would not continue.[34] They would return when sure that they would be free. Starr thought that, if necessary, these refugees might be used in building the much desired Pacific Railroad to divert them from the North.[35]

[32] Eaton, *Grant, Lincoln and the Freedmen*, p. 38.

[33] *Ibid.*, p. 39.

[34] Starr, *What shall be done with the People of Color in the United States*, p. 25; Ward, *Contrabands*, pp. 3, 4.

[35] It is said that Lincoln suggested colonizing the contrabands in South America.

There was little ground for this apprehension, in fact, if their readjustment and development in the contraband camps could be considered an indication of what the Negroes would eventually do. Taking all things into consideration, most unbiased observers felt that blacks in the camps deserved well of their benefactors.[36] According to Levi Coffin, these contrabands were, in 1864, disposed of as follows: "In military services as soldiers, laundresses, cooks, officers' servants and laborers in the various staff departments, 41,150; in cities, on plantations and in freedmen's villages and cared for, 72,500. Of these 62,300 were entirely self-supporting, just as any industrial class anywhere else, as planters, mechanics, barbers, hackmen and draymen, conducting enterprises on their own responsibility or working as hired laborers." The remaining 10,200 received subsistence from the government. 3,000 of these were members of families whose heads were carrying on plantations, and had undertaken cultivation of 4,000 acres of cotton, pledging themselves to pay the government for their subsistence from the first income of the crop. The other 7,200 included the paupers, that is, all Negroes over and under the self-supporting age, the crippled and sick in hospitals. This class, however, instead of being unproductive, had then under cultivation 500 acres of corn, 790 acres of vegetables, and 1,500 acres of cotton, besides working at wood chopping and other industries. There were reported in the aggregate over 100,000 acres of cotton under cultivation, 7,000 acres of which were leased and cultivated by blacks. Some Negroes were managing as many as 300 or 400 acres each.[37] Statistics showing exactly how much the numbers of contrabands in the various branches of the service increased are wanting, but in view of the fact that the few thousand soldiers here given increased to about 200,000 before the close of the Civil War, the other numbers must have been considerable, if they all grew the least proportionately.

Much industry was shown among these refugees. Under this new system they acquired the idea of ownership, and of the security of wages and learned to see the fundamental difference between freedom and slavery. Some Yankees, however, seeing that they did less work than did laborers in the North, considered them lazy, but the lack of industry was customary in the South and a river should not be expected to rise higher than its source. One of their superintendents said that they worked well without being urged, that there was among them a public opinion against idleness, which answered for discipline, and that those put to work with soldiers labored longer and did the

[37] Levi Coffin, *Reminiscences*, p. 671.

nicer parts. ''In natural tact and the faculty of
getting a livelihood,'' says the same writer, ''the
contrabands are inferior to the Yankees, but
quite equal to the mass of southern population.''[38] The Negroes also showed capacity to
organize labor and use capital in the promotion
of enterprises. Many of them purchased land
and cultivated it to great profit both to the community and to themselves. Others entered the
service of the government as mechanics and
contractors, from the employment of which some
of them realized handsome incomes.

The more important development, however,
was that of manhood. This was best observed
in their growing consciousness of rights, and
their readiness to defend them, even when en-
croached upon by members of the white race.
They quickly learned to appreciate freedom and
exhibited evidences of manhood in their desire
for the comforts and conveniences of life. They
readily purchased articles of furniture within
their means, bringing their home equipment up
to the standard of that of persons similarly cir-
cumstanced. The indisposition to labor was
overcome ''in a healthy nature by instinct and
motives of superior forces, such as love of life,
the desire to be clothed and fed, the sense of
security derived from provision for the future,
the feeling of self-respect, the love of family
and children and the convictions of duty.''[39]

[38] *Atlantic Monthly*, XII, p. 309.
[39] *Ibid.*, XII, pp. 310–311.

These enterprises, begun in doubt, soon ceased to be a bare hope or possibility. They became during the war a fruition and a consummation, in that they produced Negroes ''who would work for a living and fight for freedom.'' They were, therefore, considered ''adapted to civil society.'' They had ''shown capacity for knowledge, for free industry, for subordination to law and discipline, for soldierly fortitude, for social and family relations, for religious culture and aspiration. These qualities,'' said the observer, ''when stirred, and sustained by the incitements and rewards of a just society, and combining with the currents of our continental civilization, will, under the guidance of a benevolent Providence which forgets neither them nor us, make them a constantly progressive race; and secure them ever after from the calamity of another enslavement, and ourselves from the worst calamity of being their oppressors.''[40]

It is clear that these smaller numbers of Negroes under favorable conditions could be easily adjusted to a new environment. When, however, all Negroes were declared free there set in a confused migration which was much more of a problem. The first thing the Negro did after realizing that he was free was to roam over the country to put his freedom to a test. To do this, according to many writers, he fre-

[40] *Ibid.*, p. 311.

quently changed his name, residence, employment and wife, sometimes carrying with him from the plantation the fruits of his own labor. Many of them easily acquired a dog and a gun and were disposed to devote their time to the chase until the assistance in the form of mules and land expected from the government materialized. Their emancipation, therefore, was interpreted not only as freedom from slavery but from responsibility.[41]   Where they were going they did not know but the towns and cities became very attractive to them.

Speaking of this upheaval in Virginia, Eckenrode says that many of them roamed over the country without restraint.[42]   "Released from their accustomed bonds," says Hall, "and filled with a pleasing, if not vague, sense of uncontrolled freedom, they flocked to the cities with little hope of obtaining remunerative work. Wagon loads of them were brought in from the country by the soldiers and dumped down to shift for themselves."[43]   Referring to the proclamation of freedom, in Georgia, Thompson asserts that their most general and universal response was to pick up and leave the home place to go somewhere else, preferably to a town. The lure of the city was strong to the blacks, appealing to their social natures, to their inherent love

[41] Hamilton, *Reconstruction in North Carolina*, pp. 156, 157.
[42] Eckenrode, *Political History of Virginia during the Reconstruction*, p. 42.
[43] Hall, *Andrew Johnson*, p. 258.

for a crowd."[44] Davis maintains that thousands of the 70,000 Negroes in Florida crowded into the Federal military camps and into towns upon realizing that they were free.[45] According to Ficklen, the exodus of the slaves from the neighboring plantations of Louisiana into Baton Rouge, Carrollton and New Orleans was so great as to strain the resources of the Federal authorities to support them. Ten thousand poured into New Orleans alone.[46] Fleming records that upon leaving their homes the blacks collected in gangs at the cross roads, in the villages and towns, especially near the military posts. The towns were filled with crowds of blacks who left their homes with absolutely nothing, "thinking that the government would care for them, or more probably, not thinking at all."[47]

The portrayal of these writers of this phase of Reconstruction history contains a general truth, but in some cases the picture is overdrawn. The student of history must bear in mind that practically all of our histories of that period are based altogether on the testimony of prejudiced whites and are written from their point of view. Some of these writers have aimed to exaggerate the vagrancy of the blacks

[44] Thompson, *Reconstruction in Georgia*, p. 44.
[45] Davis, *Reconstruction in Florida*, p. 341.
[46] Ficklen, *History of Reconstruction in Louisiana*, p. 118.
[47] Fleming, *The Civil War and Reconstruction in Alabama*, p. 271.

to justify the radical procedure of the whites in dealing with it. The Negroes did wander about thoughtlessly, believing that this was the most effective way to enjoy their freedom. But nothing else could be expected from a class who had never felt anything but the heel of oppression. History shows that such vagrancy has always followed the immediate emancipation of a large number of slaves. Many Negroes who flocked to the towns and army camps, moreover, had like their masters and poor whites seen their homes broken up or destroyed by the invading Union armies. Whites who had never learned to work were also roaming and in some cases constituted marauding bands.[48]

There was, moreover, an actual drain of laborers to the lower and more productive lands in Mississippi and Louisiana.[49] This developed later into a more considerable movement toward the Southwest just after the Civil War, the exodus being from South Carolina, Georgia, Alabama and Mississippi to Louisiana, Arkansas and Texas. Here was the pioneering spirit, a going to the land of more economic opportunities. This slow movement continued from about 1865 to 1875, when the development of the numerous railway systems gave rise to land speculators who induced whites and blacks to go west and southwest. It was a migration of in-

[48] Thompson, *Reconstruction in Georgia*, p. 69.
[49] *Ibid.*, p. 69.

dividuals, but it was reported that as many as 35,000 Negroes were then persuaded to leave South Carolina and Georgia for Arkansas and Texas.[50]

The usual charge that the Negro is naturally migratory is not true. This impression is often received by persons who hear of the thousands of Negroes who move from one place to another from year to year because of the desire to improve their unhappy condition. In this there is no tendency to migrate but an urgent need to escape undesirable conditions. In fact, one of the American Negroes' greatest shortcomings is that they are not sufficiently pioneering. Statistics show that the whites have more inclination to move from State to State than the Negro. To prove this assertion,[51] Professor William O. Scroggs has shown that, in 1910, 16.6 per cent of the Negroes had moved to some other State than that in which they were born, while during the same period 22.4 per cent of the whites had done the same.[52]

The South, however, was not disposed to look at the vagrancy of the ex-slaves so philosophically. That section had been devastated by

[50] This exodus became considerable again in 1888 and 1889 and the Negro population has continued in this direction of plentitude of land including not only Arkansas and Texas but Louisiana and Oklahoma, all which received in this way by 1900 about 200,000 Negroes.

[51] *American Journal of Political Economy*, XXII, pp. 10, 40.

[52] *Ibid.*, XXV, p. 1038.

war and to rebuild these waste places reliable labor was necessary. Legislatures of the slave States, therefore, immediately after the close of the war, granted the Negro nominal freedom but enacted measures of vagrancy and labor so as to reduce the Negro again almost to the status of a slave. White magistrates were given wide discretion in adjudging Negroes vagrants.[53] Negroes had to sign contracts to work. If without what was considered a just cause the Negro left the employ of a planter, the former could be arrested and forced to work and in some sections with ball and chain. If the employer did not care to take him back he could be hired out by the county or confined in jail. Mississippi, Louisiana and South Carolina had further drastic features. By local ordinance in Louisiana every Negro had to be in the service of some white person, and by special laws of South Carolina and Mississippi the Negro became subject to a master almost in the same sense in which he was prior to emancipation.[54] These laws, of course, convinced the government of the United States that the South had not yet decided to let slavery go and for that reason military rule and Congressional Reconstruction followed. In this respect the South did itself a great injury, for many of the provisions of the black codes, especially the vagrancy

[53] Mecklin, *Black Codes.*
[54] Dunning, *Reconstruction,* pp. 54, 59, 110.

laws, were unnecessary. Most Negroes soon
realized that freedom did not mean relief from
responsibility and they quickly settled down to
work after a rather protracted and exciting
holiday.[55]

During the last year of and immediately after
the Civil War there set in another movement,
not of a large number of Negroes but of the intelligent class who had during years of residence
in the North enjoyed such advantages of contact and education as to make them desirable
and useful as leaders in the Reconstruction of
the South and the remaking of the race. In
their tirades against the Carpet-bag politicians
who handled the Reconstruction situation so
much to the dissatisfaction of the southern
whites, historians often forget to mention also
that a large number of the Negro leaders who
participated in that drama were also natives or
residents of Northern States.

Three motives impelled these blacks to go
South. Some had found northern communities
so hostile as to impede their progress, many
wanted to rejoin relatives from whom they had
been separated by their flight from the land of
slavery, and others were moved by the spirit of
adventure to enter a new field ripe with all sorts
of opportunities. This movement, together with
that of migration to large urban communities,
largely accounts for the depopulation and the

[55] DuBois, *Freedmen's Bureau.*

consequent decline of certain colored communities in the North after 1865.

Some of the Negroes who returned to the South became men of national prominence. William J. Simmons, who prior to the Civil War was carried from South Carolina to Pennsylvania, returned to do religious and educational work in Kentucky. Bishop James W. Hood, of the African Methodist Episcopal Zion Church, went from Connecticut to North Carolina to engage in similar work. Honorable R. T. Greener, the first Negro graduate of Harvard, went from Philadelphia to teach in the District of Columbia and later to be a professor in the University of South Carolina. F. L. Cardoza, educated at the University of Edinburgh, returned to South Carolina and became State Treasurer. R. B. Elliot, born in Boston and educated in England, settled in South Carolina from which he was sent to Congress.

John M. Langston was taken to Ohio and educated but came back to Virginia his native State from which he was elected to Congress. J. T. White left Indiana to enter politics in Arkansas, becoming State Senator and later commissioner of public works and internal improvements. Judge Mifflin Wister Gibbs, a native of Philadelphia, purposely settled in Arkansas where he served as city judge and Register of United States Land Office. T. Morris Chester, of Pittsburgh, finally made his way to Louisiana where he served with distinction as a lawyer and held the position of Brigadier-General in charge of the Louisiana State Guards under the Kellogg government. Joseph Carter Corbin, who was taken from Virginia to be educated at Chillicothe, Ohio, went later to Arkansas where he served as chief clerk in the post office at Little Rock and later as State Superintendent of Schools. Pinckney Benton Stewart Pinchback, who moved north for education and opportunity, returned to enter politics in Louisiana, which honored him with several important positions among which was that of Acting Governor.

CHAPTER VII

HAVING come through the halcyon days of the Reconstruction only to find themselves reduced almost to the status of slaves, many Negroes deserted the South for the promising west to grow up with the country. The immediate causes were doubtless political. *Bulldozing,* a rather vague term, covering all such crimes as political injustice and persecution, was the source of most complaint. The abridgment of the Negroes' rights had affected them as a great calamity. They had learned that voting is one of the highest privileges to be obtained in this life and they wanted to go where they might still exercise that privilege. That persecution was the main cause was disputed, however, as there were cases of Negroes migrating from parts where no such conditions obtained. Yet some of the whites giving their version of the situation admitted that violent methods had been used so to intimidate the Negroes as to compel them to vote according to the dictation of the whites. It was also learned that the *bulldozers* concerned in dethroning the non-taxpaying blacks were an impecunious and irresponsible group themselves, led by men of the wealthy class.[1]

Coming to the defense of the whites, some said that much of the persecution with which the blacks were afflicted was due to the fear of Negro uprisings, the terror of the days of slavery. The whites, however, did practically nothing to remove the underlying causes. They did not encourage education and made no efforts to cure the Negroes of faults for which slavery itself was to be blamed and consequently could not get the confidence of the blacks. The races tended rather to drift apart. The Negroes lived in fear of reenslavement while the whites believed that the war between the North and South would soon be renewed. Some Negroes thinking likewise sought to go to the North to be among friends. The blacks, of course, had come so to regard southern whites as their enemies as to render impossible a voluntary division in politics.

Among the worst of all faults of the whites was their unwillingness to labor and their tendency to do mischief.[2] As there were so many to live on the labor of the Negroes they were reduced to a state a little better than that of bondage. The master class was generally unfair to the blacks. No longer responsible for them as slaves, the planters endeavored after the war to

[1] *Atlantic Monthly*, LXIV, p. 222; *Nation*, XXVIII, pp. 242, 386.

[2] Thompson, *Reconstruction in Georgia*, p. 69.

get their labor for nothing. The Negroes themselves had no land, no mules, no presses nor cotton gins, and they could not acquire sufficient capital to obtain these things. They were made victims of fraud in signing contracts which they could not understand and had to suffer the consequent privations and want aggravated by robbery and murder by the Ku Klux Klan.[3] The murder of Negroes was common throughout the South and especially in Louisiana. In 1875, General Sheridan said that as many as 3,500 persons had been killed and wounded in that State, the great majority of whom being Negroes; that 1,884 were killed and wounded in 1868, and probably 1,200 between 1868 and 1875. Frightful massacres occurred in the parishes of Bossier, Catahoula, Saint Bernard, Grant and Orleans. As most of these murders were for political reasons, the offenders were regarded by their communities as heroes rather than as criminals. A massacre of Negroes began in the parish of St. Landry on the 28th of September and continued for three days, resulting in the death of from 300 to 400. Thirteen captives were taken from the jail and shot and as many as twenty-five dead bodies were found burned in the woods. There broke out in the parish of Boissier another three-day riot during which two hundred Negroes were massacred. More than forty blacks were killed in the parish of

3 Williams, *History of the Negro Race*, II, p. 375.

Caddo during the following month. In fact, the number of murders, maimings and whippings during these months aggregated over one thousand.[4] The result was that the intelligent Negroes were either intimidated or killed so that the illiterate masses of Negro voters might be ordered to refrain from voting the Republican ticket to strengthen the Democrats or be subjected to starvation through the operation of the mischievous land tenure and credit system. What was not done in 1868 to overthrow the Republican regime was accomplished by a renewed and extended use of such drastic measures throughout the South in 1876.

Certain whites maintained, however, that the unrest was due to the work of radical politicians at the North, who had sent their emissaries south to delude the Negroes into a fever of migration. Some said it was a scheme to force the nomination of a certain Republican candidate for President in 1880. Others laid it to the charge of the defeated white and black Republicans who had been thrown from power by the whites upon regaining control of the reconstructed States.[5] A few insisted that a speech delivered by Senator Windom in 1879 had given stimulus to the migration.[6] Many southerners said that speculators in Kansas had adopted

---

[4] Williams, *History of the Negro Race*, II, p. 374.

[5] *American Journal of Social Science*, XI, p. 34.

[6] *Ibid.*, XI, p. 33.

this plan to increase the value of their land. Then there were other theories as to the fundamental causes, each consisting of a charge of one political faction that some other had given rise to the movement, varying according as they were Bourbons, conservatives, native white Republicans, carpet-bag Republicans, or black Republicans.

Impartial observers, however, were satisfied that the movement was spontaneous to the extent that the blacks were ready and willing to go. Probably no more inducement was offered them than to other citizens among whom land companies sent agents to distribute literature. But the fundamental causes of the unrest were economic, for since the Civil War race troubles have never been sufficient to set in motion a large number of Negroes. The discontent resulted from the land-tenure and credit systems, which had restored slavery in a modified form.[7]

After the Civil War a few Negroes in those parts, where such opportunities were possible, invested in real estate offered for sale by the impoverished and ruined planters of the conquered commonwealths. When, however, the Negroes lost their political power, their property was seized on the plea for delinquent taxes and they were forced into the ghetto of towns and cities, as it became a crime punishable by social

[7] *Nation*, XXVIII, pp. 242, 386.

proscription to sell Negroes desirable residences.
The aim was to debase all Negroes to the status
of menial labor in conformity with the usual
contention of the South that slavery is the normal condition of the blacks.[8]
Most of the land of the South, however, always remained as large tracts held by the planters of cotton, who never thought of alienating it
to the Negroes to make them a race of small
farmers. In fact, they had not the means to
make extensive purchases of land, even if the
planters had been disposed to transfer it. Still
subject to the experimentation of white men, the
Negroes accepted the plan of paying them
wages; but this failed in all parts except in the
sugar district, where the blacks remained contented save when disturbed by political movements. They then tried all systems of working
on shares in the cotton districts; but this was
finally abandoned because the planters in some
cases were not able to advance the Negro tenant
supplies, pending the growth of the crop, and
some found the Negro too indifferent and lazy
to make the partnership desirable. Then came
the renting system which during the Reconstruction period was general in the cotton districts. This system threw the tenant on his own
responsibility and frequently made him the vic-
tim of his own ignorance and the rapacity of the
white man. As exorbitant prices were charged

[8] Williams, *History of the Negro Race*, II, p. 378.

for rent, usually six to ten dollars an acre for
land worth fifteen to thirty dollars an acre, the
Negro tenant not only did not accumulate anything but had reason to rejoice at the end of the
year, if he found himself out of debt.[9]

Along with this went the credit system which
furnished the capstone of the economic structure
so harmful to the Negro tenant. This system
made the Negroes dependent for their living on
an advance of supplies of food, clothing or tools
during the year, secured by a lien on the crop
when harvested. As the Negroes had no chance
to learn business methods during the days of
slavery, they fell a prey to a class of loan sharks,
harpies and vampires, who established stores
everywhere to extort from these ignorant tenants by the mischievous credit system their
whole income before their crops could be gathered.[10] Some planters who sympathized with
the Negroes brought forward the scheme of pro-
tecting them by advancing certain necessities at
more reasonable prices. As the planter himself,
however, was subject to usury, the scheme did
not give much relief. The Negroes' crop, therefore, when gathered went either to the merchant
or to the planter to pay the rent; for the merchant's supplies were secured by a mortgage on
the tenant's personal property and a pledge of
the growing crop. This often prevented Negro

[9] *Atlantic Monthly*, LXIV, p. 225.
[10] *Ibid.*, p. 226.

laborers in the employ of black tenants from getting their wages at the end of the year, for, although the laborer had also a lien on the growing crop, the merchant and the planter usually had theirs recorded first and secured thereby the support of the law to force the payment of their claims. The Negro tenant then began the year with three mortages, covering all he owned, his labor for the coming year and all he expected to acquire during that twelvemonth. He paid ''one-third of his product for the use of the land, he paid an exorbitant fee for recording the contract by which he paid his pound of flesh; he was charged two or three times as much as he ought to pay for ginning his cotton; and, finally, he turned over his crop to be eaten up in commissions, if any was still left to him.''[11]

The worst of all results from this iniquitous system was its effect on the Negroes themselves. It made the Negroes extravagant and unscrupulous. Convinced that no share of their crop would come to them when harvested, they did not exert themselves to produce what they could. They often abandoned their crops before harvest, knowing that they had already spent them. In cases, however, where the Negro tenants had acquired mules, horses or tools upon which the speculator had a mortgage, the blacks were actually bound to their landlords to secure the property. It was soon evident that in the end the

[11] *Atlantic Monthly*, LXIV, p. 224.

white man himself was the loser by this evil system. There appeared waste places in the country. Improvements were wanting, land lay idle for lack of sufficient labor, and that which was cultivated yielded a diminishing return on account of the ignorance and improvidence of those tilling it. These Negroes as a rule had lost the ambition to become landowners, preferring to invest their surplus money in personal effects; and in the few cases where the Negroes were induced to undertake the buying of land, they often tired of the responsibility and gave it up.[12]

There began in the spring of 1879, therefore, an emigration of the Negroes from Louisiana and Mississippi to Kansas. For some time there was a stampede from several river parishes in Louisiana and from counties just opposite them in Mississippi. It was estimated that from five to ten thousand left their homes before the movement could be checked. Persons of influence soon busied themselves in showing the blacks the necessity for remaining in the South and those who had not then gone or prepared to go were persuaded to return to the plantations. This lull in the excitement, however, was merely temporary, for many Negroes had merely returned home to make more extensive preparations for leaving the following spring. The movement was accelerated by the

[12] *The Atlantic Monthly*, XLIV, p. 223.

work of two Negro leaders of some note, Moses Singleton, of Tennessee, the self-styled Moses of the Exodus; and Henry Adams, of Louisiana, who credited himself with having organized for this purpose as many as 98,000 blacks.

Taking this movement seriously a convention of the leading whites and blacks was held at Vicksburg, Mississippi, on the sixth of May, 1879. This body was controlled mainly by unsympathetic but diplomatic whites. General N. R. Miles, of Yazoo County, Mississippi, was elected president and A. W. Crandall, of Louisiana, secretary. After making some meaningless but eloquent speeches the convention appointed a committee on credentials and adjourned until the following day. On reassembling Colonel W. L. Nugent, chairman of the the committee, presented a certain preamble and resolutions citing causes of the exodus and suggesting remedies. Among the causes, thought he, were: "the low price of cotton and the partial failure of the crop, the irrational system of planting adopted in some sections whereby labor was deprived of intelligence to direct it and the presence of economy to make it profitable, the vicious system of credit fostered by laws permitting laborers and tenants to mortgage crops before they were grown or even planted; the apprehension on the part of many colored people produced by insidious reports circulated among them that their civil and political rights were endangered or were likely to be; the hurtful and false rumors diligently disseminated, that by emigrating to Kansas the Negroes would obtain lands, mules and money from the government without cost to themselves, and become independent forever."[13]

Referring to the grievances and proposing a redress, the committee admitted that errors had been committed by the whites and blacks alike, as each in turn had controlled the government of the States there represented. The committee believed that the interests of planters and laborers, landlords and tenants were identical; that they must prosper or suffer together; and that it was the duty of the planters and landlords of the State there represented to devise and adopt some contract by which both parties would receive the full benefit of labor governed by intelligence and economy. The convention affirmed that the Negro race had been placed by the constitution of the United States and the States there represented, and the laws thereof, on a plane of absolute equality with the white race; and declared that the Negro race should be accorded the practical enjoyment of all civil and political rights guaranteed by the said constitutions and laws. The convention pledged itself to use whatever of power and influence it possessed to protect the Negro race against all dangers in respect to the fair expression of their

13 *The Vicksburg Daily Commercial,* May 6, 1879.

wills at the polls, which they apprehended might result from fraud, intimidation or *bulldozing* on the part of the whites. And as there could be no liberty of action without freedom of thought, they demanded that all elections should be fair and free and that no repressive measures should be employed by the Negroes "to deprive their own race in part of the fullest freedom in the exercise of the highest right of citizenship."[14]

The committee then recommended the abolition of the mischievous credit system, called upon the Negroes to contradict false reports as to crimes of the whites against them and, after considering the Negroes' right to emigrate, urged that they proceed about it with reason. Ex-Governor Foote, of Mississippi, submitted a plan to establish in every county a committee, composed of men who had the confidence of both whites and blacks, to be auxiliary to the public authorities, to listen to complaints and arbitrate, advise, conciliate or prosecute, as each case should demand. But unwilling to do more than make temporary concessions, the majority rejected Foote's plan.[15]

The whites thought also to stop the exodus by inducing the steamboat lines not to furnish the emigrants transportation. Negroes were also detained by writs obtained by preferring

14 *The Vicksburg Daily Commercial*, May 6, 1879.
15 *Ibid.*, May 6, 1879.

against them false charges. Some, who were willing to let the Negroes go, thought of importing white and Chinese labor to take their places. Hearing of the movement and thinking that he could offer a remedy, Senator D. W. Voorhees, of Indiana, introduced a resolution in the United States Senate authorizing an inquiry into the causes of the exodus.[16] The movement, however, could not be stopped and it became so widespread that the people in general were forced to give it serious thought. Men in favor of it declared their views, organized migration societies and appointed agents to promote the enterprise of removing the freedmen from the South.

Becoming a national measure, therefore, the migration evoked expressions from Frederick Douglass and Richard T. Greener, two of the most prominent Negroes in the United States. Douglass believed that the exodus was ill-timed. He saw in it the abandonment of the great principle of protection to persons and property in every State of the Union. He felt that if the Negroes could not be protected in every State, the Federal Government was shorn of its rightful dignity and power, the late rebellion had triumphed, the sovereign of the nation was an empty vessel, and the power and authority in individual States were supreme. He thought,

[16] *Congressional Record*, 46th Congress, 2d Session, Vol. X, p.

therefore, that it was better for the Negroes to stay in the South than to go North, as the South was a better market for the black man's labor. Douglass believed that the Negroes should be warned against a nomadic life. He did not see any more benefit in the migration to Kansas than he had years before in the emigration to Africa. The Negroes had a monopoly of labor at the South and they would be too insignificant in numbers to have such an advantage in the North. The blacks were then potentially able to elect members of Congress in the South but could not hope to exercise such power in other parts. Douglass believed, moreover, that this exodus did not conform to the ''laws of civilizing migration,'' as the carrying of a language, literature and the like of a superior race to an inferior; and it did not conform to the geographic laws assuring healthy migration from east to west in the same latitude, as this was from south to north, far away from the climate in which the migrants were born.[17]

The exodus of the Negroes, however, was heartily endorsed by Richard T. Greener. He did not consider it the best remedy for the lawlessness of the South but felt that it was a salutary one. He did not expect the United States to give the oppressed blacks in the South the protection they needed, as there is no abstract

[17] For a detailed statement of Douglass's views, see the *American Journal of Social Science,* XI, pp. 1–21.

limit to the right of a State to do anything. He would not encourage the Negro to lead a wandering life but in tнat instance such advice was gratuitous. Greener failed to find any analogy between African colonization and migration to the West as the former was promoted by slaveholders to remove the free Negro from the country and the other sprang spontaneously from the class considering itself aggrieved. "One led out of the country to a comparative wilderness; the other directed to a better land and larger opportunities." He did not see how the migration to the North would diminish the potentiality of the Negro in politics, for Massachusetts first elected Negroes to her General Court, Ohio had nominated a Negro representative and Illinois another. He showed also that Mr. Douglass's objection on the grounds of migrating from south to north rather than from east to west was not historical. He thought little of the advice to the Negroes to stick and fight it out, for he had evidence that the return of the unreconstructed Confederates to power in the South would for generations doom the blacks to political oppression unknown in the annals of a free country.

Greener showed foresight here in urging the Negroes to take up desirable western land before it would be preempted by foreigners. As the Swedes, Norwegians, Irish, Hebrews and others were organizing societies and raising funds to promote the migration of their needy to these lands, why should the Negroes be debarred? Greener had no apprehension as to the treatment the Negroes would receive in the West. He connected the movement too with the general welfare of the blacks, considering it a promising sign that they had learned to run from persecution. Having passed their first stage, that of appealing to philanthropists, the Negroes were then appealing to themselves.[18]

Feeling very much as Greener did, these Negroes rushed into Kansas and neighboring States in 1879. So many came that some systematic relief had to be offered. Mrs. Comstock, a Quaker lady, organized for this purpose the Kansas Freedmen's Relief Association, to raise funds and secure for them food and clothing. In this work she had the support of Governor J. P. Saint John. There was much suffering upon arriving in Kansas but relief came from various sources. During this year $40,000 and 500,000 pounds of clothing, bedding and the like were used. England contributed 50,000 pounds of goods and $8,000. In 1879, the refugees took up 20,000 acres of land and brought 3,000 under cultivation. The Relief Association at first furnished them with supplies, teams and seed, which they profitably used in the production of large crops. Desiring to establish homes, they built 300 cabins and saved $30,000 the first

[18] *American Journal of Social Science*, XI, pp. 22–35.

year. In April, 1,300 refugees had gathered
around Wyandotte alone. Up to that date
60,000 had come to Kansas, nearly 40,000 of
whom arrived in destitute condition. About
30,000 settled in the country, some on rented
lands and others on farms as laborers, leaving
about 25,000 in cities, where on account of
crowded conditions and the hard weather many
greatly suffered. Upon finding employment,
however, they all did well, most of them becoming self-supporting within one year after their
arrival, and few of them coming back to the Relief Association for aid the second time.[19]
This was especially true of those in Topeka,
Parsons and Kansas City.

The people of Kansas did not encourage the
blacks to come. They even sent messengers to
the South to advise the Negroes not to migrate
and, if they did come anyway, to provide themselves with equipment. When they did arrive,
however, they welcomed and assisted them as
human beings. Under such conditions the
blacks established five or six important colonies
in Kansas alone between 1879 and 1880. Chief
among these were Baxter Springs, Nicodemus,
Morton City and Singleton. Governor Saint
John, of Kansas, reported that they seemed to
be honest and of good habits, were certainly industrious and anxious to work, and so far as
they had been tried had proved to be faithful

[19] Williams, *History of the Negro*, II, p. 379.

and excellent laborers. Giving his observations there, Sir George Campbell bore testimony to the same report.[20] Out of these communities have come some most progressive black citizens. In consideration of their desirability their white neighbors have given them their cooperation, secured to them the advantages of democratic education, and honored a few of them with some of the most important positions in the State. Although the greater number of these blacks went to Kansas, about 5,000 of them sought refuge in other Western States. During these years, Negroes gradually invaded Indian Territory and increased the number already infiltrated into and assimilated by the Indian nations. When assured of their friendly attitude toward the Indians, the Negroes were accepted by them as equals, even during the days of slav-

[20] "In Kansas City," said Sir George Campbell, "and still more in the suburbs of Kansas proper the Negroes are much more numerous than I have yet seen. On the Kansas side they form quite a large proportion of the population. They are certainly subject to no indignity or ill usage. There the Negroes seem to have quite taken to work at trades." He saw them doing building work, both alone and assisting white men, and also painting and other tradesmen's work. On the Kansas side, he found a Negro blacksmith, with an establishment of his own. He had come from Tennessee after emancipation. He had not been back there and did not want to go. He also saw black women keeping apple stalls and engaged in other such occupations so as to leave him under the impression that in the States, which he called intermediate between black and white countries the blacks evidently had no difficulty.—See *American Journal of Social Science,* XI, pp. 32, 33.

ery when the blacks on account of the cruelties of their masters escaped to the wilderness.[21] Here we are at sea as to the extent to which this invasion and subsequent miscegenation of the black and red races extended for the reason that neither the Indians nor these migrating Negroes kept records and the United States Government has been disposed to classify all mixed breeds in tribes as Indians. Having equal opportunity among the red men, the Negroes easily succeeded. A traveler in Indian Territory in 1880 found their condition unusually favorable. The cosy homes and promising fields of these freedmen attracted his attention as striking evidences of their thrift. He saw new fences, additions to cabins, new barns, churches and schoolhouses indicating prosperity. Given every privilege which the Indians themselves enjoyed, the Negroes could not be other than contented.[22]

It was very unfortunate, however, that in 1889, when by proclamation of President Harrison the Oklahoma Territory was thrown open, the intense race prejudice of the white immigrants and the rule of the mob prevented a larger number of Negroes from settling in that promising commonwealth. Long since extensively advertised as valuable, the land of Oklahoma had become a coveted prize for the adventurous squatters invading the territory in defiance of

---

[21] *American Journal of Social Science,* XI, p. 33.
[22] *Ibid.,* XI, p. 33.

the law before it was declared open for settlement. The rush came with all the excitement of pioneer days redoubled. Stakes were set, parcels of land were claimed, cabins were constructed in an hour and towns grew up in a day.[23] Then came conflicting claims as to titles and rights of preemption culminating in fighting and bloodshed. And worst of all, with this disorderly group there developed the fixed policy of eliminating the Negroes entirely.

The Negro, however, was not entirely excluded. Some had already come into the territory and others in spite of the barriers set up continued to come.[24] With the cooperation of the Indians, with whom they easily amalgamated, they readjusted themselves and acquired sufficient wealth to rise in the economic world. Although not generally fortunate, a number of them have coal and oil lands from which they obtain handsome incomes and a few, like Sara Rector, have actually become rich. Dishonest white men with the assistance of unprincipled officials have defrauded and are still endeavoring to defraud these Negroes of their property, lending them money secured by mortgages and obtaining for themselves through the courts appointments as the Negroes' guardians. They turn out to be the robbers of the Negroes,

[23] *Spectator*, LXVII, p. 571; *Dublin Review*, CV, p. 187; *Cosmopolitan*, VII, p. 460; *Nation*, LXVIII, p. 279.

[24] According to the *United States Census, of 1910*, there are 137,612 Negroes in Oklahoma.

in case they do not live in a community where an enlightened public opinion frowns down upon this crime.

During the later eighties and the early nineties there were some other interstate movements worthy of notice here. The mineral wealth of the Appalachian mountains was being exploited. Foreigners, at first, were coming into this country in sufficiently large numbers to meet the demand; but when this supply became inadequate, labor agents appealed to the blacks in the South. Negroes then flocked to the mining districts of Birmingham, Alabama, and to East Tennessee. A large number also migrated from North Carolina and Virginia to West Virginia and some few of the same group to Southern Ohio to take the places of those unreasonable strikers who often demanded larger increases in wages than the income of their employers could permit. Many of these Negroes came to West Virginia as is evidenced by the increase in Negro population of that State. West Virginia had a Negro population of 17,980 in 1870; 25,886 in 1880; 32,690 in 1890; 43,499 in 1900; and 64,173 in 1910.[25]

[25] See *Censuses* of the United States.

CHAPTER VIII

THE MIGRATION OF THE TALENTED TENTH

IN spite of these interstate movements, the Negro still continued as a perplexing problem, for the country was unprepared to grant the race political and civil rights. Nominal equality was forced on the South at the point of the sword and the North reluctantly removed most of its barriers against the blacks. Some, still thinking, however, that the two races could not live together as equals, advocated ceding the blacks the region on the Gulf of Mexico.[1] This was branded as chimerical on the ground that, deprived of the guidance of the whites, these States would soon sink to African level and the end of the experiment would be a reconquest and a military regime fatal to the true development of American institutions.[2] Another plan proposed was the revival of the old colonization idea of sending Negroes to Africa, but this exhibited still less wisdom than the first in that it was based on the hypothesis of deporting a nation, an expense which no government would be willing to incur. There were then no physical means of transporting six or seven mil-

[1] Pike, *The Prostrate State*, pp. 3, 4.
[2] *Spectator*, LXVI, p. 113.

147

lions of people, moreover, as there would be a new born for every one the agents of colonization could deport.[3] With the deportation scheme still kept before the people by the American Colonization Society, the idea of emigration to Africa did not easily die. Some Negroes continued to emigrate to Liberia from year to year. This policy was also favored by radicals like Senator Morgan, of Alabama, who, after movements like the Ku Klux Klan had done their work of intimidating Negroes into submission to the domination of the whites, concluded that most of the race believed that there was no future for the blacks in the United States and that they were willing to emigrate. These radicals advocated the deportation of the blacks to prevent the recurrence of "Negro domination." This plan was acceptable to the whites in general also, for, unlike the consensus of opinion of today, it was then thought that the South could get along without the Negro.[4] Even newspapers like the *Charleston News and Courier,* which denounced the persecution of the Negroes, urged them to emigrate to Africa as they could not be permitted to rule over the white people. The *Minneapolis Times* wished the scheme success and

[3] Frederick Douglass pointed out this difficulty prior to the Civil War.—See John Lobb's *Life and Times of Frederick Douglass,* p. 250.

[4] Labor was then cheap in the South because of its abundance and the foreign laborer had not then been tried.

Godspeed and believed that the sooner it was carried out the better it would be for the Negroes.

Most of the influential newspapers of the country, however, urged the contrary. Citing the progress of the Negroes since emancipation to show that the blacks were doing their full share toward developing the wealth of the South, the *Indianapolis Journal* characterized as barbarism the suggestion that the government should furnish them transportation to Africa. "The ancestors of most of the Negroes now in this country," said the editor, " have doubtless been here as long as those of Senator Morgan, and their descendants are as thoroughly acclimated and have as good a right here as the Senator himself."[5] This was the opinion of all useful Negroes except Bishop H. M. Turner, who endorsed Morgan's plan by advocating the emigration of one fourth of the blacks to Africa. The editor of the *Chicago Record-Herald* entreated Turner to temper his enthusiasm with discretion before he involved in unspeakable disaster any more of his trustful compatriots.

Speaking more plainly to the point, the editor of the *Philadelphia North American* said that the true interest of the South was to accommodate itself to changed conditions and that the

[5] During these years Senator Morgan of Alabama was endeavoring to arouse the people of the country so as to make this a matter of national concern.

duty of the freedmen lies in making themselves worth more in the development of the South than they were as chattels. Although recognizing the disabilities and hardships of the South both to the whites and the blacks, he could not believe that the elimination of the Negroes would, if practicable, give relief.[6] The *Boston Herald* inquired whether it was worth while to send away a laboring population in the absence of whites to take its place and referred to the misfortunes of Spain which undertook to carry out such a scheme. Speaking the real truth, *The Milwaukee Journal* said that no one needed to expect any appreciable decrease in the black population through any possible emigration, no matter how successful it might be. "The Negro," said the editor, "is here to stay and our institutions must be adapted to comprehend him and develop his possibilities." *The Colored American,* then the leading Negro organ of thought in the United States, believed that the Negroes should be thankful to Senator Morgan for his attitude on emigration, because he might succeed in deporting to Africa those Negroes who affect to believe that this is not their home and the more quickly we get rid of such foolhardy people the better it will be for the stalwart of the race.[7]

A number of Negroes, however, under the in-

[6] *Public Opinion,* XVIII, p. 371.
[7] *Ibid.,* XVIII, p. 371.

spiration of leaders[8] like Bishop H. M. Turner, did not feel that the race had a fair chance in the United States. A few of them emigrated to Wapimo, Mexico; but, becoming dissatisfied with the situation there, they returned to their homes in Georgia and Alabama in 1895. The coming of the Negroes into Mexico caused suspicion and excitement. A newspaper, *El Tiempo,* which had been denouncing lynching in the United States, changed front when these Negroes arrived in that country.

Going in quest of new opportunities and desiring to reenforce the civilization of Liberia, 197 other Negroes sailed from Savannah, Georgia, for Liberia, March 19, 1895. Commending this step, the *Macon Telegraph* referred to their action as a rebellion against the social laws which govern all people of this country. This organ further said that it was the outcome of a feeling which has grown stronger and stronger year by year among the Negroes of the Southern States and which will continue to grow with the increase of education and intelligence among them. The editor conceded that they had an opportunity to better their material condition and acquire wealth here but contended that they had no chance to rise out of the peasant class. *The Memphis Commercial Appeal* urged the building of a large Negro nation in Africa as practicable and desirable, for it was "more

8 Simmons, *Men of Mark,* p. 817.

and more apparent that the Negro in this country must remain an alien and a disturber," because there was "not and can never be a future for him in this country." *The Florida Times Union* felt that this colonization scheme, like all others, was a fraud. It referred to the Negro's being carried to the land of plenty only to find out that there, as everywhere else in the world, an existence must be earned by toil and that his own old sunny southern home is vastly the better place.[9]

Only a few intelligent Negroes, however, had reached the position of being contented in the South. The Negroes eliminated from politics could not easily bring themselves around to thinking that they should remain there in a state of recognized inferiority, especially when during the eighties and nineties there were many evidences that economic as well as political conditions would become worse. The exodus treated in the previous chapter was productive of better treatment for the Negroes and an increase in their wages in certain parts of the South but the migration, contrary to the expectations of many, did not bcome general. Actual prosperity was impossible even if the whites had been willing to give the Negro peasants a fair chance. The South had passed through a disastrous war, the effects of which so blighted the hopes of its citizens in the economic world that

[9] *Public Opinion*, XVIII, pp. 370–371.

their land seemed to pass, so to speak, through a dark age. There was then little to give the man far down when the one to whom he of necessity looked for employment was in his turn bled by the merchant or the banker of the larger cities, to whom he had to go for extensive credits.[10]

Southern planters as a class, however, had not much sympathy for the blacks who had once been their property and the tendency to cheat them continued, despite the fact that many farmers in the course of time extricated themselves from the clutches of the loan sharks. There were a few Negroes who, thanks to the honesty of certain southern gentlemen, succeeded in acquiring considerable property in spite of their handicaps.[11] They yielded to the white man's control in politics, when it seemed that it meant either to abandon that field or die, and devoted themselves to the accumulation of wealth and the acquisition of education.

This concession, however, did not satisfy the radical whites, as they thought that the Negro might some day return to power. Unfortunately, therefore, after the restoration of the control of the State governments to the master class, there swept over these commonwealths a

[10] Because of these conditions the last fifty years has been considered by some writers as a ''dark age,'' for the South.

[11] The Negroes are now said to be worth more than a billion dollars. Most of this property is in the hands of southern Negroes.

wave of hostile legislation demanded by the poor
white uplanders determined to debase the blacks
to the status of the free Negroes prior to the Civil
War.[12] The Negroes have, therefore, been disfranchised in most reconstructed States, deprived of the privilege of serving in the State
militia, segregated in public conveyances, and
excluded from public places of entertainment.
They have, moreover, been branded by public
opinion as pariahs of society to be used for
exploitation but not to be encouraged to expect
that their status can ever be changed so as to
destroy the barriers between the races in their
social and political relations.

This period has been marked also by an effort
to establish in the South a system of peonage
not unlike that of Mexico, a sort of involuntary
servitude in that one is considered legally bound
to serve his master until a debt contracted is
paid. Such laws have been enacted in Florida,
Alabama, Georgia, Mississippi, North Carolina
and South Carolina. No such distinction in law
has been able to stand the constitutional test of
the United States courts as was evidenced by
the decision of the Supreme Court in 1911 de-
claring the Alabama law unconstitutional.[13]
But the planters of the South, still a law unto
themselves, have maintained actual slavery in

[12] *American Law Review*, XL, pp. 29, 52, 205, 227, 354, 381,
547, 590, 695, 758, 865, 905.

[13] No. 300.—Original, October Term, 1910.

sequestered districts where public opinion against peonage is too weak to support federal authorities in exterminating it.[14] The Negroes themselves dare not protest under penalty of persecution and the peon concerned usually accepts his lot like that of a slave. Some years ago it was commonly reported that in trying to escape, the persons undertaking it often fail and suffer death at the hands of the planter or of murderous mobs, giving as their excuse, if any be required, that the Negro is a desperado or some other sort of criminal.

Unfortunately this reaction extended also to education. Appropriations to public schools for Negroes diminished from year to year and when there appeared practical leaders with their sane plan for industrial education the South ignorantly accepted this scheme as a desirable subterfuge for seeming to support Negro education and at the same time directing the development of the blacks in such a way that they would never become the competitors of the white people. This was not these educators' idea but the South so understood it and in effecting the readjustment, practically left the Negroes out of the pale of the public school systems. Consequently, there has been added to the Negroes' misfortunes, in the South, that of being unable to obtain liberal education at public expense, although they themselves, as the largest

14 Hershaw, *Peonage,* pp. 10–11.

consumers in some parts, pay most of the taxes appropriated to the support of schools for the youth of the other race.[15]

The South, moreover, has adopted the policy of a more general intimidation of the Negroes to keep them down. The lynching of the blacks, at first for assaults on white women and later for almost any offense, has rapidly developed as an institution. Within the past fifty years[16] there have been lynched in the South about 4,000 Negroes, many of whom have been publicly burned in the daytime to attract crowds that usually enjoy such feats as the tourney of the Middle Ages. Negroes who have the courage to protest against this barbarism have too often been subjected to indignities and in some cases forced to leave their communities or suffer the fate of those in behalf of whom they speak. These crimes of white men were at first kept secret but during the last two generations the culprits have become known as heroes, so popular has it been to murder Negroes. It has often been discovered also that the officers of these communities take part in these crimes and the worst of all is that politicians like Tillman, Blease and Vardaman glory in recounting the noble deeds of those who deserve so well of their countrymen for making the soil red with the Ne-

[15] These facts are well brought out by Dr. Thomas Jesse Jones' recent report on Negro Education.

[16] This is based on reports published annually in the *Chicago Tribune.*

groes' blood rather than permit the much feared Africanization of southern institutions.[17]

In this harassing situation the Negro has hoped that the North would interfere in his behalf, but, with the reactionary Supreme Court of the United States interpreting this hostile legislation as constitutional in conformity with the demands of prejudiced public opinion, and with the leaders of the North inclined to take the view that after all the factions in the South must be left alone to fight it out, there has been nothing to be expected from without. Matters too have been rendered much worse because the leaders of the very party recently abandoning the freedmen to their fate, aggravated the critical situation by first setting the Negroes against their former masters, whom they were taught to regard as their worst enemies whether they were or not.

The last humiliation the Negroes have been forced to submit to is that of segregation. Here the effort has been to establish a ghetto in cities and to assign certain parts of the country to Negroes engaged in farming. It always happens, of course, that the best portion goes to the whites and the least desirable to the blacks, although the promoters of the segregation maintain that both races are to be treated equally. The ultimate aim is to prevent the Negroes of means from figuring conspicuously in aristo-

[17] This is the boast of southern men of this type when speaking to their constituents or in Congress.

cratic districts where they may be brought into
rather close contact with the whites. Negroes
see in segregation a settled policy to keep them
down, no matter what they do to elevate themselves. The southern white man, eternally
dreading the miscegenation of the races, makes
the life, liberty and happiness of individuals
second to measures considered necessary to prevent this so-called evil that this enviable civilization, distinctly American, may not be destroyed. The United States Supreme Court in
the decision of the Louisville segregation case
recently declared these segregation measures
unconstitutional.[18]

These restrictions have made the progress of
the Negroes more of a problem in that directed
toward social distinction, the Negroes have been
denied the helpful contact of the sympathetic
whites. The increasing race prejudice forces
the whites to restrict their open dealing with
the blacks to matters of service and business,
maintaining even then the bearing of one in a
sphere which the Negroes must not penetrate.
The whites, therefore, never seeing the blacks as
they are, and the blacks never being able to
learn what the whites know, are thrown back on
their own initiative, which their life as slaves
could not have permitted to develop. It makes
little difference that the Negroes have been free
a few decades. Such freedom has in some parts

[18] *Report*, October Term, 1917.

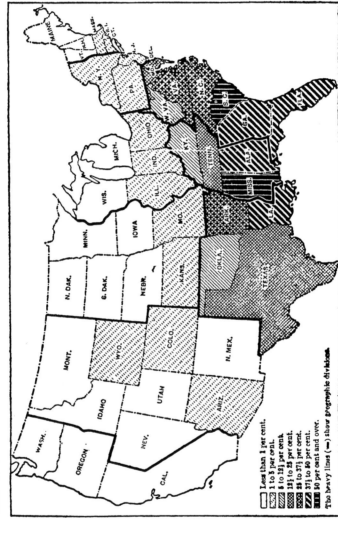

MAP SHOWING THE PER CENT OF NEGROES IN TOTAL POPULATION, BY STATES: 1910.

(Map 2, Bulletin 129, The United States Bureau of the Census.)

been tantamount to slavery, and so far as contact with the superior class is concerned, no better than that condition; for under the old regime certain slaves did learn much by close association with their masters.[19]

For these reasons there has been since the exodus to the West a steady migration of Negroes from the South to points in the North. But this migration, mainly due to political changes, has never assumed such large proportions as in the case of the more significant movements due to economic causes, for, as the accompanying map shows, most Negroes are still in the South. When we consider the various classes migrating, however, it will be apparent that to understand the exodus of the Negroes to the North, this longer drawn out and smaller movement must be carefully studied in all its ramifications. It should be noted that unlike some of the other migrations it has not been directed to any particular State. It has been from almost all Southern States to various parts of the North and especially to the largest cities.[20]

What classes then have migrated? In the first place, the Negro politicians, who, after the restoration of Bourbon rule in the South, found themselves thrown out of office and often humil-

[19] This danger has been often referred to when the Negroes were first emancipated.—See *Spectator*, LXVI, p. 113.

[20] Compare the Negro population of Northern States as given in the census of 1800 with the same in 1900.

iated and impoverished, had to find some way out of the difficulty. Some few have been relieved by sympathetic leaders of the Republican party, who secured for them federal appointments in Washington. These appointments when sometimes paying lucrative salaries have been given as a reward to those Negroes who, although dethroned in the South, remain in touch with the remnant of the Republican party there and control the delegates to the national conventions nominating candidates for President. Many Negroes of this class have settled in Washington.[21] In some cases, the observer witnesses the pitiable scene of a man once a prominent public functionary in the South now serving in Washington as a messenger or a clerk.

The well-established blacks, however, have not been so easily induced to go. The Negroes in business in the South have usually been loath to leave their people among whom they can acquire property, whereas, if they go to the North, they have merely political freedom with no assurance of an opportunity in the economic world. But not a few of these have given themselves up to unrelenting toil with a view to accumulating sufficient wealth to move North and live thereafter on the income from their investments. Many of this class now spend some of their time in the North to educate their children.

[21] Hart, *Southern South*, pp. 171, 172.

But they do not like to have these children who have been under refining influences return to the South to suffer the humiliation which during the last generation has been growing more and more aggravating. Endeavoring to carry out their policy of keeping the Negro down, southerners too often carefully plan to humiliate the progressive and intelligent blacks and in some cases form mobs to drive them out, as they are bad examples for that class of Negroes whom they desire to keep as menials.[22]

There are also the migrating educated Negroes. They have studied history, law and economics and well understand what it is to get the rights guaranteed them by the constitution. The more they know the more discontented they become. They cannot speak out for what they want. No one is likely to second such a protest, not even the Negroes themselves, so generally have they been intimidated. The more outspoken they become, moreover, the more necessary is it for them to leave, for they thereby destroy their chances to earn a livelihood. White men in control of the public schools of the South see to it that the subserviency of the Negro teachers employed be certified beforehand. They dare not complain too much about equipment and salaries even if the per capita appro-

[22] This is based on the experience of the writer and others whom he has interviewed.

priation for the education of the Negroes be one
fourth of that for the whites.[28]

In the higher institutions of learning, especially the State schools, it is exceptional to find
a principal who has the confidence of the Negroes. The Negroes will openly assert that he
is in the pay of the reactionary whites, whose
purpose is to keep the Negro down; and the
incumbent himself will tell his board of regents
how much he is opposed by the Negroes because
he labors for the interests of the white race.
Out of such sycophancy it is easily explained
why our State schools have been so ineffective
as to necessitate the sending of the Negro youth
to private institutions maintained by northern
philanthropy. Yet if an outspoken Negro
happens to be an instructor in a private school
conducted by educators from the North, he has to
be careful about contending for a square deal;
for, if the head of his institution does not suggest to him to proceed conservatively, the mob
will dispose of the complainant.[23] Physicians,
lawyers and preachers who are not so economic-
ally dependent as teachers can exercise no more
freedom of speech in the midst of this triumphant rule of the lawless.

A large number of educated Negroes, therefore, have on account of these conditions been

[28] In his report on Negro education Dr. Thomas Jesse Jones
has shown this to be an actual fact.

[23] Negroes applying for positions in the South have the situation set before them so as to know what to expect.

DIAGRAM SHOWING THE NEGRO POPULATION OF NORTHERN AND WESTERN CITIES IN 1900 AND THE EXTENT TO WHICH IT INCREASED BY 1910.

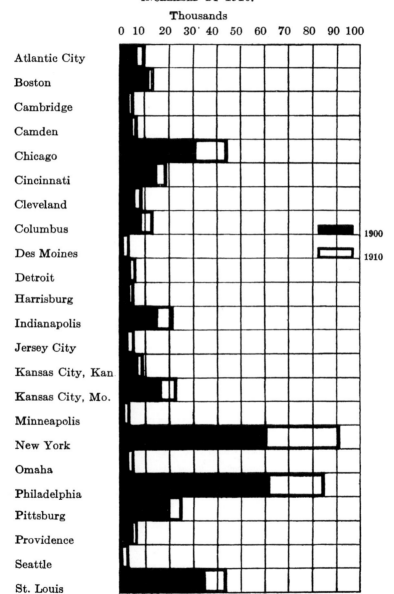

compelled to leave the South. Finding in the North, however, practically nothing in their line to do, because of the proscription by race prejudice and trades unions, many of them lead the life of menials, serving as waiters, porters, butlers and chauffeurs. While in Chicago, not long ago, the writer was in the office of a graduate of a colored southern college, who was showing his former teacher the picture of his class. In accounting for his classmates in the various walks of life he reported that more than one third of them were settled to the occupation of Pullman porters.

The largest number of Negroes who have gone North during this period, however, belong to the intelligent laboring class. Some of them have become discontented for the very same reasons that the higher classes have tired of oppression in the South, but the larger number of them have gone North to improve their economic condition. Most of these have migrated to the large cities in the East and Northwest, such as Philadelphia, New York, Indianapolis, Pittsburgh, Cleveland, Columbus, Detroit and Chicago. To understand this problem in its urban aspects the accompanying diagram showing the increase in the Negro population of northern cities during the first decade of this century will be helpful.

Some of these Negroes have migrated after careful consideration; others have just happened to go north as wanderers; and a still larger number on the many excursions to the cities conducted by railroads during the summer months. Sometimes one excursion brings to Chicago two or three thousand Negroes, two thirds of whom never go back. They do not often follow the higher pursuits of labor in the North but they earn more money than they have been accustomed to earn in the South. They are attracted also by the liberal attitude of some whites, which, although not that of social equality, gives the Negroes a liberty in northern centers which leads them to think that they are citizens of the country.[24]

This shifting in the population has had an unusually significant effect on the black belt. Frederick Douglass advised the Negroes in 1879 to remain in the South where they would be in sufficiently large numbers to have political power,[25] but they have gradually scattered from the black belt so as to diminish greatly their chances ever to become the political force they formerly were in this country. The Negroes once had this possibility in South Carolina, Georgia, Alabama, Mississippi and Louisiana and, had the process of Africanization prior to the Civil War had a few decades longer to do its work, there would not have been any doubt as to the ultimate preponderance of the

[24] The *American Journal of Political Economy*, XXV, p. 1040.
[25] The *Journal of Social Science*, XI, p. 16.

1 9 1 0

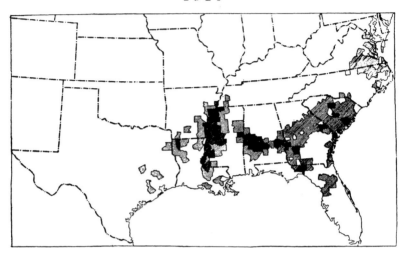

1 8 8 0

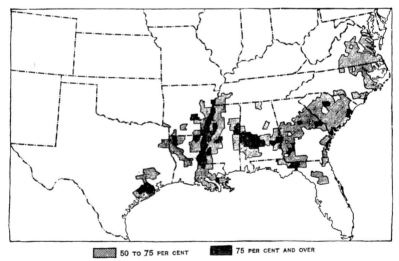

50 to 75 per cent   75 per cent and over

(Maps 3 and 4, Bulletin 129, U. S. Bureau of the Census.)

1 9 0 0

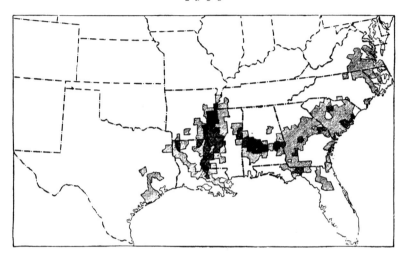

1 8 6 0

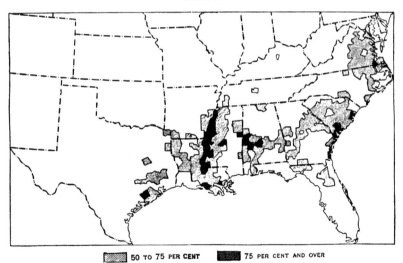

50 TO 75 PER CENT   75 PER CENT AND OVER

(Maps 5 and 6, Bulletin 129, U. S. Bureau of the Census.)

Negroes in those commonwealths. The tendencies of the black population according to the censuses of the United States and especially that of 1910, however, show that the chances for the control of these State governments by Negroes no longer exist except in South Carolina and Mississippi.[26] It has been predicted, therefore, that, if the same tendencies continue for the next fifty years, there will be even few counties in which the Negroes will be in a majority. All of the Southern States except Arkansas showed a proportionate increase of the white population over that of the black between 1900 and 1910, while West Virginia and Oklahoma with relatively small numbers of blacks showed, for reasons stated elsewhere, an increase in the Negro population. Thus we see coming to pass something like the proposed plan of Jefferson and other statesmen who a hundred years ago advocated the expansion of slavery to lessen the evil of the institution by distributing its burdens.[27]

The migration of intelligent blacks, however, has been attended with several handicaps to the race. The large part of the black population is in the South and there it will stay for decades to come. The southern Negroes, therefore, have been robbed of their due part of the talented tenth. The educated blacks have had no con-

[26] *American Economic Review,* IV, pp. 281–292.
[27] Ford edition of *Jefferson's Writings,* X, p. 231.

stituency in the North and, consequently, have been unable to realize their sweetest dreams of the land of the free. In their new home the enlightened Negro must live with his light under a bushel. Those left behind in the South soon despair of seeing a brighter day and yield to the yoke. In the places of the leaders who were wont to speak for their people, the whites have raised up Negroes who accept favors offered them on the condition that their lips be sealed up forever on the rights of the Negro.

This emigration too has left the Negro subject to other evils. There are many first-class Negro business men in the South, but although there were once progressive men of color, who endeavored to protect the blacks from being plundered by white sharks and harpies there have arisen numerous unscrupulous Negroes who have for a part of the proceeds from such jobbery associated themselves with ill-designing white men to dupe illiterate Negroes. This trickery is brought into play in marketing their crops, selling them supplies, or purchasing their property. To carry out this iniquitous plan the persons concerned have the protection of the law, for while Negroes in general are imposed upon, those engaged in robbing them have no cause to fear.

CHAPTER IX

THE EXODUS DURING THE WORLD WAR

WITHIN the last two years there has been a steady stream of Negroes into the North in such large numbers as to overshadow in its results all other movements of the kind in the United States. These Negroes have come largely from Alabama, Tennessee, Florida, Georgia, Virginia, North Carolina, Kentucky, South Carolina, Arkansas and Mississippi. The given causes of this migration are numerous and complicated. Some untruths centering around this exodus have not been unlike those of other migrations. Again we hear that the Negroes are being brought North to fight organized labor,[1] and to carry doubtful States for the Republicans.[2] These numerous explanations themselves, however, give rise to doubt as to the fundamental cause.

Why then should the Negroes leave the South? It has often been spoken of as the best place for them. There, it is said, they have made unusual strides forward. The progress of the Negroes in the South, however, has in no sense been general, although the land owned by Negroes in the

[1] *New York Times*, Sept. 5, 9, 28, 1916.
[2] *Ibid.*, Oct. 18, 28; Nov. 5, 7, 12, 15; Dec. 4, 9, 1916.

country and the property of thrifty persons of their race in urban communities may be extensive. In most parts of the South the Negroes are still unable to become landowners or successful business men. Conditions and customs have reserved these spheres for the whites. Generally speaking, the Negroes are still dependent on the white people for food and shelter. Although not exactly slaves, they are yet attached to the white people as tenants, servants or dependents. Accepting this as their lot, they have been content to wear their lord's cast-off clothing, and live in his ramshackled barn or cellar. In this unhappy state so many have settled down, losing all ambition to attain a higher station. The world has gone on but in their sequestered sphere progress has passed them by.

What then is the cause? There have been *bulldozing,* terrorism, maltreatment and what not of persecution; but the Negroes have not in large numbers wandered away from the land of their birth. What the migrants themselves think about it, goes to the very heart of the trouble. Some say that they left the South on account of injustice in the courts, unrest, lack of privileges, denial of the right to vote, bad treatment, oppression, segregation or lynching. Others say that they left to find employment, to secure better wages, better school facilities, and

8 *The New Orleans Times Picayune,* March 26, 1914.

better opportunities to toil upward.[9] Southern white newspapers unaccustomed to give the Negroes any mention but that of criminals have said that the Negroes are going North because they have not had a fair chance in the South and that if they are to be retained there, the attitude of the whites toward them must be changed. Professor William O. Scroggs, of Louisiana State University, considers as causes of this exodus "the relatively low wages paid farm labor, an unsatisfactory tenant or crop-sharing system, the boll weevil, the crop failure of 1916, lynching, disfranchisement, segregation, poor schools, and the monotony, isolation and drudgery of farm life." Professor Scroggs, however, is wrong in thinking that the persecution of the blacks has little to do with the migration for the reason that during these years when the treatment of the Negroes is decidedly better they are leaving the South. This does not mean that they would not have left before, if they had had economic opportunities in the North. It is highly probable that the Negroes would not be leaving the South today, if they were treated as men, although there might be numerous opportunities for economic improvement in the North.[10]

The immediate cause of this movement was the suffering due to the floods aggravated by

[9] *The Crisis,* July, 1917.

[10] *American Journal of Political Economy,* XXX, p. 1040.

the depredations of the boll weevil. Although generally mindful of our welfare, the United States Government has not been as ready to build levees against a natural enemy to property as it has been to provide fortifications for warfare. It has been necessary for local communities and State governments to tax themselves to maintain them. The national government, however, has appropriated to the purpose of facilitating inland navigation certain sums which have been used in doing this work, especially in the Mississippi Valley. There are now 1,538 miles of levees on both sides of the Mississippi from Cape Girardeau to the passes. These levees, of course, are still inadequate to the security of the planters against these inundations. Carrying 406 million tons of mud a year, the river becomes a dangerous stream subject to change, abandoning its old bed to cut for itself a new channel, transferring property from one State to another, isolating cities and leaving once useful levees marooned in the landscape like old Indian mounds or overgrown intrenchments.[3]

This valley has, therefore, been frequently visited with disasters which have often set the population in motion. The first disastrous floods came in 1858 and 1859, breaking many of the levees, the destruction of which was practically completed by the floods of 1865 and 1869. There is an annual rise in the stream, but since

[3] *The World's Work*, XX, p. 271.

1874 this river system has fourteen times devastated large areas of this section with destructive floods. The property in this district depreciated in value to the extent of about 400 millions in ten years. Farmers from this section, therefore, have at times moved west with foreigners to take up public lands.

The other disturbing factor in this situation was the boll weevil, an interloper from Mexico in 1892. The boll weevil is an insect about one fourth of an inch in length, varying from one eighth to one third of an inch with a breadth of about one third of the length. When it first emerges it is yellowish, then becomes grayish brown and finally assumes a black shade. It breeds on no other plant than cotton and feeds on the boll. This little animal, at first attacked the cotton crop in Texas. It was not thought that it would extend its work into the heart of the South so as to become of national consequence, but it has, at the rate of forty to one hundred sixty miles annually, invaded all of the cotton district except that of the Carolinas and Virginia. The damage it does, varies according to the rainfall and the harshness of the winter, increasing with the former and decreasing with the latter. At times the damage has been to the extent of a loss of 50 per cent. of the crop, estimated at 400,000 bales of cotton annually, about 4,500,000 bales since the invasion or $250,000,000 worth of cotton.[4] The out-

4 *The World's Work,* XX, p. 272.

put of the South being thus cut off, the planter has less income to provide supplies for his black tenants and, the prospects for future production being dark, merchants accustomed to give them credit have to refuse. This, of course, means financial depression, for the South is a borrowing section and any limitation to credit there blocks the wheels of industry. It was fortunate for the Negro laborers in this district that there was then a demand for labor in the North when this condition began to obtain.

This demand was made possible by the cutting off of European immigration by the World War, which thereby rendered this hitherto uncongenial section an inviting field for the Negro. The Negroes have made some progress in the North during the last fifty years, but despite their achievements they have been so handicapped by race prejudice and proscribed by trades unions that the uplift of the race by economic methods has been impossible. The European immigrants have hitherto excluded the Negroes even from the menial positions. In the midst of the drudgery left for them, the blacks have often heretofore been debased to the status of dependents and paupers. Scattered through the North too in such small numbers, they have been unable to unite for social betterment and mutual improvement and naturally too weak to force the community to respect their wishes as could be done by a large group with some political or economic power. At present, however, Negro laborers, who once went from city to city, seeking such employment as trades unions left to them, can work even as skilled laborers throughout the North.[5] Women of color formerly excluded from domestic service by foreign maids are now in demand. Many mills and factories which Negroes were prohibited from entering a few years ago are now bidding for their labor. Railroads cannot find help to keep their property in repair, contractors fall short of their plans for failure to hold mechanics drawn into the industrial boom and the United States Government has had to advertise for men to hasten the preparation for war.

Men from afar went south to tell the Negroes of a way of escape to a more congenial place. Blacks long since unaccustomed to venture a few miles from home, at once had visions of a promised land just a few hundred miles away. Some were told of the chance to amass fabulous riches, some of the opportunities for education and some of the hospitality of the places of amusement and recreation in the North. The migrants then were soon on the way. Railway stations became conspicuous with the presence of Negro tourists, the trains were crowded to full capacity and the streets of northern cities

[5] *New York Times,* March 29, April 7, 9, May 30 and 31, 1917.

were soon congested with black laborers seeking
to realize their dreams in the land of unusual
opportunity.

Employment agencies, recently multiplied to
meet the demand for labor, find themselves unable to cope with the situation and agents sent
into the South to induce the blacks by offers of
free transportation and high wages to go north,
have found it impossible to supply the demand
in centers where once toiled the Poles, Italians
and the Greeks formerly preferred to the Negroes.[6] In other words, the present migration
differs from others in that the Negro has opportunity awaiting him in the North whereas
formerly it was necessary for him to make a
place for himself upon arriving among enemies.
The proportion of those returning to the South,
therefore, will be inconsiderable.

Becoming alarmed at the immensity of this
movement the South has undertaken to check it.
To frighten Negroes from the North southern
newspapers are carefully circulating reports
that many of them are returning to their native
land because of unexpected hardships.[7] But
having failed in this, southerners have compelled employment agents to cease operations
there, arrested suspected employers and, to pre-

[6] *Survey*, XXXVII, pp. 569–571 and XXXVIII, pp. 27, 226,
331, 428; *Forum*, LVII, p. 181; *The World's Work*, XXXIV,
pp. 135, 314–319; *Outlook*, CXVI, pp. 520–521; *Independent*,
XCI, pp. 53–54.

[7] *The Crisis*, 1917.

vent the departure of the Negroes, imprisoned
on false charges those who appear at stations to
leave for the North. This procedure could not
long be effective, for by the more legal and clandestine methods of railway passenger agents the
work has gone forward. Some southern communities have, therefore, advocated drastic
legislation against labor agents, as was suggested in Louisiana in 1914, when by operation
of the Underwood Tariff Law the Negroes
thrown out of employment in the sugar district
migrated to the cotton plantations.[8]

One should not, however, get the impression
that the majority of the Negroes are leaving
the South. Eager as these Negroes seem to go,
there is no unanimity of opinion as to whether
migration is the best policy. The sycophant,
toady class of Negroes naturally advise the
blacks to remain in the South to serve their
white neighbors. The radical protagonists of
the equal-rights-for-all element urge them to
come North by all means. Then there are the
thinking Negroes, who are still further divided.
Both divisions of this element have the interests
of the race at heart, but they are unable to agree
as to exactly what the blacks should now do.
Thinking that the present war will soon be over
and that consequently the immigration of foreigners into this country will again set in and
force out of employment thousands of Negroes
who have migrated to the North, some of the

most representative Negroes are advising their fellows to remain where they are. The most serious objection to this transplantation is that it means for the Negroes a loss of land, the rapid acquisition of which has long been pointed to as the best evidence of the ability of the blacks to rise in the economic world. So many Negroes who have by dint of energy purchased small farms yielding an increasing income from year to year, are now disposing of them at nominal prices to come north to work for wages. Looking beyond the war, however, and thinking too that the depopulation of Europe during this upheaval will render immigration from that quarter for some years an impossibility, other thinkers urge the Negroes to continue the migration to the North, where the race may be found in sufficiently large numbers to wield economic and political power.

Great as is the dearth of labor in the South, moreover, the Negro exodus has not as yet caused such a depression as to unite the whites in inducing the blacks to remain in that section. In the first place, the South has not yet felt the worst effects of this economic upheaval as that part of the country has been unusually aided by the millions which the United States Government is daily spending there. Furthermore, the poor whites are anxious to see the exodus of their competitors in the field of labor. This leaves the capitalists at their mercy, and in keeping with their domineering attitude, they will be able to handle the labor situation as they desire. As an evidence of this fact we need but note the continuation of mob rule and lynching in the South despite the preachings against it of the organs of thought which heretofore winked at it. This terrorism has gone to an unexpected extent. Negro farmers have been threatened with bodily injury, unless they leave certain parts.

The southerner of aristocratic bearing will say that only the shiftless poor whites terrorize the Negroes. This may be so, but the truth offers little consolation when we observe that most white people in the South are of this class; and the tendency of this element to put their children to work before they secure much education does not indicate that the South will soon experience that general enlightenment necessary to exterminate these survivals of barbarism. Unless the upper classes of the whites can bring the mob around to their way of thinking that the persecution of the Negro is prejudicial to the interests of all, it is not likely that mob rule will soon cease and the migration to this extent will be promoted rather than retarded.

It is unfortunate for the South that the growing consciousness of the Negroes has culminated at the very time they are most needed. Finally heeding the advice of agricultural experts to reconstruct its agricultural system, the South has learned in the school of bitter experience to depart from the plan of producing the single cotton crop. It is now raising food-stuffs to make that section self-supporting without reducing the usual output of cotton. With the increasing production in the South, therefore, more labor is needed just at the very time it is being drawn to centers in the North. The North being an industrial and commercial section has usually attracted the immigrants, who will never fit into the economic situation in the South because they will not accept the treatment given Negroes. The South, therefore, is now losing the only labor which it can ever use under present conditions.

Where these Negroes are going is still more interesting. The exodus to the west was mainly directed to Kansas and neighboring States, the migration to the Southwest centered in Oklahoma and Texas, pioneering Negro laborers drifted into the industrial district of the Appalachian highland during the eighties and nineties and the infiltration of the discontented talented tenth affected largely the cities of the North. But now we are told that at the very time the mining districts of the North and West are being filled with blacks the western planters are supplying their farms with them and that into some cities have gone sufficient skilled and unskilled Negro workers to increase the black population more than one hundred per cent. Places in the North, where the black population has not only not increased but even decreased in recent years, are now receiving a steady influx of Negroes. In fact, this is a nation-wide migration affecting all parts and all conditions.

Students of social problems are now wondering whether the Negro can be adjusted in the North. Many perplexing problems must arise. This movement will produce results not unlike those already mentioned in the discussion of other migrations, some of which we have evidence of today. There will be an increase in race prejudice leading in some communities to actual outbreaks as in Chester and Youngstown and probably to massacres like that of East St. Louis, in which participated not only well-known citizens but the local officers and the State militia. The Negroes in the North are in competition with white men who consider them not only strike breakers but a sort of inferior individuals unworthy of the consideration which white men deserve. And this condition obtains even where Negroes have been admitted to the trades unions.

Negroes in seeking new homes in the North, moreover, invade residential districts hitherto exclusively white. There they encounter prejudice and persecution until most whites thus disturbed move out determined to do whatever they can to prevent their race from suffering from further depreciation of property and the disturbance of their community life. Lawlessness has followed, showing that violence may under certain conditions develop among some classes anywhere rather than reserve itself for vigilance committees of primitive communities. It has brought out too another aspect of lawlessness in that it breaks out in the North where the numbers of Negroes are still too small to serve as an excuse for the terrorism and lynching considered necessary in the South to keep the Negroes down.

The maltreatment of the Negroes will be nationalized by this exodus. The poor whites of both sections will strike at this race long stigmatized by servitude but now demanding economic equality. Race prejudice, the fatal weakness of the Americans, will not so soon abate although there will be advocates of fraternity, equality and liberty required to reconstruct our government and rebuild our civilization in conformity with the demands of modern efficiency by placing every man regardless of his color wherever he may do the greatest good for the greatest number.

The Negroes, however, are doubtless going to the North in sufficiently large numbers to make themselves felt. If this migration falls short of establishing in that section Negro colonies large enough to wield economic and political power, their state in the end will not be any better than that of the Negroes already there. It is to these large numbers alone that we must look for an agent to counteract the development of race feeling into riots. In large numbers the blacks will be able to strike for better wages or concessions due a rising laboring class and they will have enough votes to defeat for reelection those officers who wink at mob violence or treat Negroes as persons beyond the pale of the law.

The Negroes in the North, however, will get little out of the harvest if, like the blacks of Reconstruction days, they unwisely concentrate their efforts on solving all of their problems by electing men of their race as local officers or by sending a few members even to Congress as is likely in New York, Philadelphia and Chicago within the next generation. The Negroes have had representatives in Congress before but they were put out because their constituency was uneconomic and politically impossible. There was nothing but the mere letter of the law behind the Reconstruction Negro officeholder and the thus forced political recognition against public opinion could not last any longer than natural forces for some time thrown out of gear by unnatural causes could resume the usual line of procedure.

It would be of no advantage to the Negro race today to send to Congress forty Negro Representatives on the pro rata basis of numbers, especially if they happened not to be exceptionally well qualified. They would remain in Congress only so long as the American white people could devise some plan for eliminating them as they did during the Reconstruction period. Near as the world has approached real democracy, history gives no record of a permanent government conducted on this basis. Interests have always been stronger than numbers. The Negroes in the North, therefore, should not on the eve of the economic revolution follow the advice of their misguided and misleading race leaders who are diverting their attention from their actual welfare to a specialization in politics. To concentrate their efforts on electing a few Negroes to office wherever the blacks are found in the majority, would exhibit the narrowness of their oppressors. It would be as unwise as the policy of the Republican party of setting aside a few insignificant positions like that of Recorder of Deeds, Register of the Treasury and Auditor of the Navy as segregated jobs for Negroes. Such positions have furnished a nucleus for the large, worthless, office-seeking class of Negroes in Washington, who have established the going of the people of the city toward pretence and sham.

The Negroes should support representative men of any color or party, if they stand for a square deal and equal rights for all. The new Negroes in the North, therefore, will, as so many of their race in New York, Philadelphia

and Chicago are now doing, ally themselves
with those men who are fairminded and consid-
erate of the man far down, and seek to embrace
their many opportunities for economic progress,
a foundation for political recognition, upon
which the race must learn to build. Every race
in the universe must aspire to becoming a factor
in politics; but history shows that there is no
short route to such success. Like other despised
races beset with the prejudice and militant opposition of self-styled superiors, the Negroes
must increase their industrial efficiency, improve
their opportunities to make a living, develop the
home, church and school, and contribute to art,
literature, science and philosophy to clear the
way to that political freedom of which they
cannot be deprived.

The entire country will be benefited by this
upheaval. It will be helpful even to the South.
The decrease in the black population in those
communities where the Negroes outnumber the
whites will remove the fear of *Negro domination,* one of the causes of the backwardness of
the South and its peculiar civilization. Many
of the expensive precautions which the southern
people have taken to keep the Negroes down,
much of the terrorism incited to restrain the
blacks from self-assertion will no longer be considered necessary; for, having the excess in numbers on their side, the whites will finally rest assured that the Negroes may be encouraged with-

out any apprehension that they may develop enough power to subjugate or embarrass their former masters.

The Negroes too are very much in demand in the South and the intelligent whites will gladly give them larger opportunities to attach them to that section, knowing that the blacks, once conscious of their power to move freely throughout the country wherever they may improve their condition, will never endure hardships like those formerly inflicted upon the race. The South is already learning that the Negro is the most desirable laborer for that section, that the persecution of Negroes not only drives them out but makes the employment of labor such a problem that the South will not be an attractive section for capital. It will, therefore, be considered the duty of business men to secure protection to the Negroes lest their ill-treatment force them to migrate to the extent of bringing about a stagnation of their business.

The exodus has driven home the truth that the prosperity of the South is at the mercy of the Negro. Dependent on cheap labor, which the bulldozing whites will not readily furnish, the wealthy southerners must finally reach the position of regarding themselves and the Negroes as having a community of interests which each must promote. ''Nature itself in those States,'' Douglass said, ''came to the rescue of the Negro. He had labor, the South wanted it,

and must have it or perish. Since he was free
he could then give it, or withhold it; use it where
he was, or take it elsewhere, as he pleased. His
labor made him a slave and his labor could, if
he would, make him free, comfortable and independent. It is more to him than either fire,
sword, ballot boxes or bayonets. It touches the
heart of the South through its pocket."[11]
Knowing that the Negro has this silent weapon
to be used against his employer or the community, the South is already giving the race better
educational facilities, better railway accommo-
dations, and will eventually, if the advocacy of
certain southern newspapers be heeded, grant
them political privileges. Wages in the South,
therefore, have risen even in the extreme south-
western States, where there is an opportunity to
import Mexican labor. Reduced to this ex-
tremity, the southern aristocrats have begun to
lose some of their race prejudice, which has not
hitherto yielded to reason or philanthropy.

Southern men are telling their neighbors that
their section must abandon the policy of treating the Negroes as a problem and construct a
program for recognition rather than for repres-
sion. Meetings are, therefore, being held to
find out what the Negro wants and what may be
done to keep them contented. They are told that
the Negro must be elevated not exploited, that
to make the South what it must needs be, the co-

[11] *American Journal of Social Science*, XI, p. 4.

operation of all is needed to train and equip the men of all races for efficiency. The aim of all then must be to reform or get rid of the unfair proprietors who do not give their tenants a fair division of the returns from their labor. To this end the best whites and blacks are urged to come together to find a working basis for a systematic effort in the interest of all.

To say that either the North or the South can easily become adjusted to this change is entirely too sanguine. The North will have a problem. The Negroes in the northern city will have much more to contend with than when settled in the rural districts or small urban centers. Forced by restrictions of real estate men into congested districts, there has appeared the tendency toward further segregation. They are denied social contact, are sagaciously separated from the whites in public places of amusement and are clandestinely segregated in public schools in spite of the law to the contrary. As a consequence the Negro migrant often finds himself with less friends than he formerly had. The northern man who once denounced the South on account of its maltreatment of the blacks gradually grows silent when a Negro is brought next door. There comes with the movement, therefore, the difficult problem of housing.

Where then must the migrants go. They are not wanted by the whites and are treated with contempt by the native blacks of the northern cities, who consider their brethren from the South too criminal and too vicious to be tolerated. In the average progressive city there has heretofore been a certain increase in the number of houses through natural growth, but owing to the high cost of materials, high wages, increasing taxation and the inclination to invest money in enterprises growing out of the war, fewer houses are now being built, although Negroes are pouring into these centers as a steady stream. The usual Negro quarters in northern centers of this sort have been filled up and the overflow of the black population scattered throughout the city among white people. Old warehouses, store rooms, churches, railroad cars and tents have been used to meet these demands.

A large per cent of these Negroes are located in rooming houses or tenements for several families. The majority of them cannot find individual rooms. Many are crowded into the same room, therefore, and too many into the same bed. Sometimes as many as four and five sleep in one bed, and that may be placed in the basement, dining-room or kitchen where there is neither adequate light nor air. In some cases men who work during the night sleep by day in beds used by others during the night. Some of their houses have no water inside and have toilets on the outside without sewerage connections. The cooking is often done by coal or wood stoves or kerosene lamps. Yet the rent runs high although the houses are generally out of repair and in some cases have been condemned by the municipality. The unsanitary conditions in which many of the blacks are compelled to live are in violation of municipal ordinances. Furthermore, because of the indiscriminate employment by labor agents and the dearth of labor requiring the acceptance of almost all sorts of men, some disorderly and worthless Negroes have been brought into the North. On the whole, however, these migrants are not lazy, shiftless and desperate as some predicted that they would be. They generally attend church, save their money and send a part of their savings regularly to their families. They do not belong to the class going North in quest of whiskey. Mr. Abraham Epstein, who has written a valuable pamphlet setting forth his researches in Pittsburgh, states that the migrants of that city do not generally imbibe and most of those who do, take beer only.[12] Out of four hundred and seventy persons to whom he propounded this question, two hundred and ten or forty-four per cent of them were total abstainers. Seventy per cent of those having families do not drink at all.

With this congestion, however, have come serious difficulties. Crowded conditions give rise to vice, crime and disease. The prevalence of vice has not been the rule but tendencies,

12 Epstein, *The Negro Migrant in Pittsburgh.*

which better conditions in the South restrained
from developing, have under these undesirable
conditions been given an opportunity to grow.
There is, therefore, a tendency toward the
crowding of dives, assembling on the corners
of streets and the commission of petty offences
which crowd them into the police courts. One
finds also sometimes a congestion in houses of
dissipation and the carrying of concealed weapons. Law abiding on the whole, however, they
have not experienced a wave of crime. The
chief offences are those resulting from the
saloons and denizens of vice, which are furnished by the community itself.

Disease has been one of their worst enemies,
but reports on their health have been exag-
gerated. On account of this sudden change of
the Negroes from one climate to another and the
hardships of more unrelenting toil, many of
them have been unable to resist pneumonia,
bronchitis and tuberculosis. Churches, rescue
missions and the National League on Urban
Conditions Among Negroes have offered relief in some of these cases. The last-named organization is serving in large cities as a sort of
clearing house for such activities and as means
of interpreting one race to the other. It has
now eighteen branches in cities to which this migration has been directed. Through a local
worker these migrants are approached, properly placed and supervised until they can adjust

themselves to the community without apparent embarrassment to either race. The League has been able to handle the migrants arriving by extending the work so as to know their movements beforehand.

The occupations in which these people engage will throw further light on their situation. About ninety per cent of them do unskilled labor. Only ten per cent of them do semi-skilled or skilled labor. They serve as common laborers, puddlers, mold-setters, painters, carpenters, bricklayers, cement workers and machinists. What the Negroes need then is that sort of freedom which carries with it industrial opportunity and social justice. This they cannot attain until they be permitted to enter the higher pursuits of labor. Two reasons are given for failure to enter these: first, that Negro labor is unstable and inefficient; and second, that white men will protest. Organized labor, however, has done nothing to help the blacks. Yet it is a fact that accustomed to the easy-going toil of the plantation, the blacks have not shown the same efficiency as that of the whites. Some employers report, however, that they are glad to have them because they are more individualistic and do not like to group. But it is not true that colored labor cannot be organized. The blacks have merely been neglected by organized labor. Wherever they have had the opportunity to do so, they have organized and stood for their rights like men. The trouble is that the trades unions are generally antagonistic to Negroes although they are now accepting the blacks in self-defense. The policy of excluding Negroes from these bodies is made effective by an evasive procedure, despite the fact that the constitutions of many of them specifically provide that there shall be no discrimination on account of race or color.

Because of this tendency some of the representatives of trades unions have asked why Negroes do not organize unions of their own. This the Negroes have generally failed to do, thinking that they would not be recognized by the American Federation of Labor, and knowing too that what their union would have to contend with in the economic world would be diametrically opposed to the wishes of the men from whom they would have to seek recognition. Organized labor, moreover, is opposed to the powerful capitalists, the only real friends the Negroes have in the North to furnish them food and shelter while their lives are often being sought by union members. Steps toward organizing Negro labor have been made in various Northern cities during 1917 and 1918.[13] The objective of this movement for the present, however, is largely that of employment.

Eventually the Negro migrants will, no doubt,

[13] Epstein, *The Negro Migrant in Pittsburgh.*

without much difficulty establish themselves
among law-abiding and industrious people of
the North where they will receive assistance.
Many persons now see in this shifting of the
Negro population the dawn of a new day, not in
making the Negro numerically dominant anywhere to obtain political power, but to secure
for him freedom of movement from section to
section as a competitor in the industrial world.
They also observe that while there may be an increase of race prejudice in the North the same
will in that proportion decrease in the South,
thus balancing the equation while giving the
Negro his best chance in the economic world
out of which he must emerge a real man with
power to secure his rights as an American
citizen.

BIBLIOGRAPHY

As the public has not as yet paid very much attention to Negro History, and has not seen a volume dealing primarily with the migration of the race in America, one could hardly expect that there has been compiled a bibliography in this special field. With the exception of what appears in Still's and Siebert's works on the *Underground Railroad* and the records of the meetings of the Quakers promoting this movement, there is little helpful material to be found in single volumes bearing on the antebellum period. Since the Civil War, however, more has been said and written concerning the movements of the Negro population. E. H. Botume's *First Days Among the Contrabands* and John Eaton's *Grant, Lincoln and the Freedmen* cover very well the period of rebellion. This is supplemented by J. C. Knowlton's *Contrabands* in the *University Quarterly*, Volume XXI, page 307, and by Edward L. Pierce's *The Freedmen at Port Royal* in the *Atlantic Monthly*, Volume XII, page 291. The exodus of 1879 is treated by J. B. Runnion in the *Atlantic Monthly*, Volume XLIV, page 222; by Frederick Douglass and Richard T. Greener in the *American Journal of Social Science*, Volume XI, page 1; by F. R. Guernsey in the *International Review*, Volume VII, page 373; by E. L. Godkin in the *Nation*, Volume XXVIII, pages 242 and 386; and by J. C. Hartzell in the *Methodist Quarterly*, Volume XXXIX, page 722. The second volume of George W. Williams's *History of the Negro Race* also contains a short chapter on the exodus of 1879. In Volume XVIII, page 370, of *Public Opinion* there is a discussion of *Negro Emigration and Deportation* as advocated by Bishop H. M. Turner and Senator Morgan of Alabama during the nineties. Professor William O. Scroggs of Louisiana University has in the *Journal of Political Economy*, Volume XXV, page 1034, an article entitled *Interstate Migration of Negro Population*. Mr. Epstein has published a helpful pamphlet, *The Negro Migrant in Pittsburgh.*

194 *A Century of Negro Migration*

Most of the material for this work, however, was collected from the various sources mentioned below.

BOOKS OF TRAVEL

BRISSOT DE WARVILLE, J. P. *New Travels in the United States of America: including the Commerce of America with Europe, particularly with Great Britain and France.* Two volumes. (London, 1794.) Gives general impressions, few details.

BUCKINGHAM, J. S. *America, Historical, Statistical, and Descriptive.* Two volumes. (New York, 1841.)

—— *Eastern and Western States of America.* Three volumes. (London and Paris, 1842.) Contains useful information.

OLMSTED, FREDERICK LAW. *A Journey in the Seaboard Slave States, with Remarks on their Economy.* (New York, 1859.)

—— *A Journey in the Back Country.* (London, 1860.)

—— *Journeys and Explorations in the Cotton Kingdom.* (London, 1861.) Olmsted was a New York farmer. He recorded a few important facts about the Negroes immediately before the Civil War.

WOOLMAN, JOHN. *Journal of John Woolman, with an Introduction by John G. Whittier.* (Boston, 1873.) Woolman traveled so extensively in the colonies that he probably knew more about the Negroes than any other Quaker of his time.

LETTERS

BOYCE, STANBURY. *Letters on the Emigration of the Negroes to Trinidad.*

JEFFERSON, THOMAS. *Letters of Thomas Jefferson to Abbé Grégoire, M. A. Julien, and Benjamin Banneker.* In *Jefferson's Works, Memorial Edition,* xii and xv. He comments on Negroes' talents.

MADISON, JAMES. *Letters to Frances Wright.* In *Madison's Works,* vol. iii, p. 396. The emancipation of Negroes is discussed.

MAY, SAMUEL JOSEPH. *The Right of the Colored People to Education.* (Brooklyn, 1883.) A collection of public letters addressed to Andrew T. Judson, remonstrating on the unjust procedure relative to Miss Prudence Crandall.

McDonogh, John. *''A Letter of John McDonogh on African Colonization addressed to the Editor of the New Orleans Commercial Bulletin.''* McDonogh was interested in the betterment of the colored people and did much to promote their mental development.

BIOGRAPHIES

Birney, William. *James G. Birney and His Times.* (New York, 1890.) A sketch of an advocate of Negro uplift.

Bowen, Clarence W. *Arthur and Lewis Tappan.* A paper read at the fiftieth anniversary of the New York Anti-Slavery Society, at the Broadway Tabernacle, New York City, October 2, 1883. An honorable mention of two friends of the Negro.

Drew, Benjamin. *A North-side View of Slavery. The Refugee: or the Narratives of Fugitive Slaves in Canada. Related by themselves, with an Account of the History and Condition of the Colored Population of Upper Canada.* (New York and Boston, 1856.)

Frothingham, O. B. *Gerritt Smith: A Biography.* (New York, 1878.)

Garrison, Francis and Wendell P. *William Lloyd Garrison, 1805–1879. The Story of his Life told by his Children.* Four volumes. (Boston and New York, 1894.) Includes a brief account of what he did for the colored people.

Hammond, C. A. *Gerritt Smith, The Story of a Noble Man's Life.* (Geneva, 1900.)

Johnson, Oliver. *William Lloyd Garrison and his Times.* (Boston, 1880. New edition, revised and enlarged, Boston, 1881.)

Mott, A. *Biographical Sketches and Interesting Anecdotes of Persons of Color; with a Selection of Pieces of Poetry.* (New York, 1826.) Some of these sketches show how ambitious Negroes succeeded in spite of opposition.

Simmons, W. J. *Men of Mark; Eminent, Progressive, and Rising, with an Introductory Sketch of the Author by Reverend Henry M. Turner.* (Cleveland, Ohio, 1891.) Accounts for the adverse circumstances under which many antebellum Negroes made progress.

AUTOBIOGRAPHIES

COFFIN, LEVI. *Reminiscences of Levi Coffin, reputed President of the Underground Railroad.* Second edition. (Cincinnati, 1880.) Contains many facts concerning Negroes.

DOUGLASS, FREDERICK. *Narrative of the Life of Frederick Douglass, as an American Slave.* Written by himself. (Boston, 1845.) Gives several cases of secret Negro movements for their own good.

—— *The Life and Times of Frederick Douglass from 1817 to 1882.* (London, 1882.) Written by himself. With an Introduction by the Right Honorable John Bright, M.P. Edited by John Loeb, F.R.G.S., of the *Christian Age.* Editor of *Uncle Tom's Story of his Life.*

HISTORIES

BANCROFT, GEORGE. *History of the United States.* Ten volumes. (Boston, 1857–1864.)

BRACKETT, JEFFREY R. *The Negro in Maryland.* Johns Hopkins University Studies. (Baltimore, 1889.)

COLLINS, LEWIS. *Historical Sketches of Kentucky.* (Maysville, Ky., and Cincinnati, Ohio, 1847.)

DUNN, J. P. *Indiana; A redemption from Slavery.* (In the American Commonwealths, vols. XII, Boston and New York, 1888.)

EVANS, W. E. *A History of Scioto County together with a Pioneer Record of Southern Ohio.* (Portsmouth, 1903.)

FARMER, SILAS. *The History of Detroit and Michigan or the Metropolis Illustrated.* A chronological encyclopedia of the past and the present including a full record of territorial days in Michigan and the annals of Wayne County. Two volumes. (Detroit, 1899.)

HARRIS, N. D. *The History of Negro Servitude in Illinois and of the Slavery Agitation in that State, 1719–1864.* (Chicago, 1904.)

HART, A. B. *The American Nation; A History, etc.* Twenty-seven volumes. (New York, 1904–1908.) The volumes which have a bearing on the subject treated in this monograph are W. A. Dunning's *Reconstruction*, F. J. Turner's *Rise of the New West*, and A. B. Hart's *Slavery and Abolition.*

HINSDALE, B. A. *The Old Northwest; with a view of the thir-teen colonies as constituted by the royal charters.* (New York, 1888.)

HOWE, HENRY. *Historical Collections of Ohio.* Contains a collection of the most interesting facts, traditions, bio-graphical sketches, anecdotes, etc., relating to its general and local history with descriptions of its counties, prin-cipal towns and villages. (Cincinnati, 1847.)

JONES, CHARLES COLCOCK, JR. *History of Georgia.* (Boston, 1883.)

MCMASTER, JOHN B. *History of the United States.* Six volumes. (New York, 1900.)

RHODES, J. F. *History of the United States from the Com-promise of 1850 to the Final Restoration of Home Rule in the South.* (New York and London, Macmillan & Com-pany, 1892–1906.)

STEINER, B. C. *History of Slavery in Connecticut.* (Johns Hopkins University Studies, 1893.)

STUVE, BERNARD, and ALEXANDER DAVIDSON. *A Complete His-tory of Illinois from 1673 to 1783.* (Springfield, 1874.)

TREMAIN, MARY M. A. *Slavery in the District of Columbia.* (University of Nebraska Seminary Papers, April, 1892.)

History of Brown County, Ohio. (Chicago, 1883.)

ADDRESSES

GARRISON, WILLIAM LLOYD. *An Address Delivered before the Free People of Color in Philadelphia, New York and other Cities during the Month of June, 1831.* (Boston, 1831.)

GRIFFIN, EDWARD DORR. *A Plea for Africa.* (New York, 1817.) A Sermon preached October 26, 1817, in the First Presbyterian Church in the City of New York before the Synod of New York and New Jersey at the Request of the Board of Directors of the African School established by the Synod. The aim was to arouse interest in colonization.

REPORTS AND STATISTICS

Special Report of the Commissioner of Education on the Im-provement of Public Schools in the District of Columbia, containing M. B. Goodwin's ''History of Schools for the

Colored Population in the District of Columbia.'' (Washington, 1871.)

Report of the Committee of Representatives of the New York Yearly Meeting of Friends upon the condition and wants of the Colored Refugees, 1862.

CLARKE, J. F. *Present Condition of the Free Colored People of the United States.* (New York and Boston, the American Antislavery Society, 1859.) Published also in the March number of the *Christian Examiner.*

Condition of the Free People of Color in Ohio. With interesting anecdotes. (Boston, 1839.)

Institute for Colored Youth. (Philadelphia, 1860–1865.) Contains a list of the officers and students.

JONES, THOMAS JESSE. *Negro Education: A study of the private and higher schools for colored people in the United States. Prepared in cooperation with the Phelps-Stokes Fund.* In two volumes. (Bureau of Education, Washington, 1917.)

Official Records of the War of Rebellion.

Report of the Condition of the Colored People of Cincinnati, 1835. (Cincinnati, 1835.)

Report of a Committee of the Pennsylvania Society of Abolition on Present Condition of the Colored People, etc., 1838. (Philadelphia, 1838.)

Statistical Inquiry into the Condition of the People of Color of the City and Districts of Philadelphia. (Philadelphia, 1849.)

Statistics of the Colored People of Philadelphia in 1859, compiled by Benj. C. Bacon. (Philadelphia, 1859.)

Statistical Abstract of the United States, 1898. Prepared by the Bureau of Statistics. (Washington, D. C., 1899.)

Statistical View of the Population of the United States, A 1790–1830. (Published by the Department of State in 1835.)

Trades of the Colored People. (Philadelphia, 1838.)

United States Censuses.

A Brief Statement of the Rise and Progress of the Testimony of Friends against Slavery and the Slave Trade. Published by direction of the Yearly Meeting held in Philadelphia in the Fourth Month, 1843. Shows the action taken by various Friends to elevate the Negroes.

A Collection of the Acts, Deliverances and Testimonies of the Supreme Judicatory of the Presbyterian Church, from its Origin in America to the Present Time. By Samuel J. Baird. (Philadelphia, 1856.)

AMERICAN CONVENTION OF ABOLITION SOCIETIES. *Minutes of the Proceedings of a Convention of Delegates from the Abolition Societies established in different Parts of the United States.* From 1794–1828.

The Annual Reports of the American and Foreign Anti-Slavery Societies, presented at New York, May 6, 1847, with the Addresses and Resolutions. From 1847–1851.

The Annual Reports of the American Anti-Slavery Society. From 1834 to 1860.

The Third Annual Report of the Managers of the New England Anti-Slavery Society presented June 2, 1835. (Boston, 1835.)

Annual Reports of the Massachusetts (or New England) Anti-Slavery Society, 1831–end.

Reports of the National Anti-Slavery Convention, 1833–end.

Reports of the American Colonization Society, 1818–1832.

Report of the New York Colonization Society, October 1, 1823. (New York, 1823.)

The Seventh Annual Report of the Colonization Society of the City of New York. (New York, 1839.)

Proceedings of the New York State Colonization Society, 1831. (Albany, 1831.)

The Eighteenth Annual Report of the Colonization Society of the State of New York. (New York, 1850.)

Minutes and Proceedings of the First Annual Convention of the People of Color. Held by Adjournment in the City of Philadelphia, from the sixth to the eleventh of June, inclusive, 1831. (Philadelphia, 1831.)

Minutes and Proceedings of the Second Annual Convention for the Improvement of the Free People of Color in these United States. Held by Adjournments in the City of Philadelphia, from the 4th to the 13th of June, inclusive, 1832. (Philadelphia, 1832.)

Minutes and Proceedings of the Third Annual Convention for the Improvement of the Free People of Color in these United States. Held by Adjournments in the City of

Philadelphia, in 1833. (New York, 1833.) These proceedings were published also in the *New York Commercial
Advertiser,* April 27, 1833.

*Minutes and Proceedings of the Fourth Annual Convention for
the Improvement of the Free People of Color in the
United States. Held by Adjournments in the Asbury
Church, New York, from the 2d to the 12th of June, 1834.*
(New York, 1834.)

*Proceedings of the Convention of the Colored Freedmen of
Ohio at Cincinnati, January 14, 1852.* (Cincinnati, Ohio,
1852.)

MISCELLANEOUS BOOKS AND PAMPHLETS

ADAMS, ALICE DANA. *The Neglected Period of Anti-Slavery
in America.* Radcliffe College Monographs No. 14. (Boston and London, 1908.) Contains some valuable facts
about the Negroes during the first three decades of the
nineteenth century.

AGRICOLA (pseudonym). *An Impartial View of the Real State
of the Black Population in the United States.* (Philadelphia, 1824.)

ALEXANDER, A. *A History of Colonization on the Western
Continent of Africa.* (Philadelphia, 1846.)

AMES, MARY. *From a New England Woman's Diary in 1865.*
(Springfield, 1906.)

*An Address to the People of North Carolina on the Evils of
Slavery, by the Friends of Liberty and Equality, 1830.*
(Greensborough, 1830.)

*An Address to the Presbyterians of Kentucky proposing a Plan
for the Instruction and Emancipation of their Slaves by
a Committee of the Synod of Kentucky.* (Newburyport,
1836.)

BALDWIN, EBENEZER. *Observations on the Physical and Moral
Qualities of our Colored Population with Remarks on the
Subject of Emancipation and Colonization.* (New Haven,
1834.)

BASSETT, J. S. *Slavery and Servitude in the Colony of North
Carolina.* (Johns Hopkins University Studies in Historical
and Political Science. Fourteenth Series, iv–v. Baltimore, 1896.)

—— *Slavery in the State of North Carolina.* (Johns Hopkins University Studies in Historical and Political Science. Series XVII., Nos. 7–8. Baltimore, 1899.)

—— *Anti-Slavery Leaders of North Carolina.* (Johns Hopkins University Studies in Historical and Political Science. Series XVI., No. 6. Baltimore, 1898.)

BENEZET, ANTHONY. *A Caution to Great Britain and Her Colonies in a Short Representation of the calamitous State of the enslaved Negro in the British Dominions.* (Philadelphia, 1784.)

—— *The Case of our Fellow-Creatures, the oppressed Africans, respectfully recommended to the serious Consideration of the Legislature of Great Britan, by the People called Quakers.* (London, 1783.)

—— *Observations on the enslaving, Importing and Purchasing of Negroes; with some Advice thereon, extracted from the Epistle of the Yearly-Meeting of the People called Quakers, held at London in the Year 1748.* (Germantown, 1760.)

—— *The Potent Enemies of America laid open: being some Account of the baneful Effects attending the Use of distilled spirituous Liquors, and the Slavery of the Negroes.* (Philadelphia.)

—— *A Short Account of that Part of Africa, inhabited by the Negroes. With respect to the Fertility of the Country; the good Disposition of many of the Natives, and the Manner by which the Slave Trade is carried on.* (Philadelphia, 1792.)

—— *Short Observations on Slavery, introductory to Some Extracts from the Writings of the Abbé Raynal, on the Important Subject.*

—— *Some Historical Account of Guinea, its Situation, Produce, and the General Disposition of its Inhabitants. With an Inquiry into the Rise and Progress of the Slave Trade, its Nature and Lamentable Effects.* (London, 1788.)

BIRNEY, JAMES G. *The American Churches, the Bulwarks of American Slavery, by an American.* (Newburyport, 1842.)

BIRNEY, WILLIAM. *James G. Birney and his Times. The Genesis of the Republican Party, with Some Account of the Abolition Movements in the South before 1828.* (New York, 1890.)

202 *A Century of Negro Migration*

BRACKETT, JEFFERY R. *The Negro in Maryland. A Study of the Institution of Slavery.* (Baltimore, Johns Hopkins University, 1889.)

BRANNAGAN, THOMAS. *A Preliminary Essay on the Oppression of the Exiled Sons of Africa, Consisting of Animadversions on the Impolicy and Barbarity of the Deleterious Commerce and Subsequent Slavery of the Human Species.* (Philadelphia: Printed for the Author by John W. Scott, 1804.)

BRANNAGAN, T. *Serious Remonstrances Addressed to the Citizens of the Northern States and their Representatives, being an Appeal to their Natural Feelings and Common Sense; Consisting of Speculations and Animadversions, on the Recent Revival of the Slave Trade in the American Republic.* (Philadelphia, 1805.)

CAMPBELL, J. V. *Political History of Michigan.* (Detroit, 1876.)

Code Noir ou Recueil d'édits, declarations et arrêts concernant la Discipline et le commerce des esclaves Nègres des isles francaises de l'Amérique (in Recueils de réglemens, édits, déclarations et arrêts, concernant le commerce, l'administration de la justice et la police des colonies françaises de l'Amérique, et les engagés avec le Code Noir, et l'addition audit code. (Paris, 1745.)

COFFIN, JOSHUA. *An Account of Some of the principal Slave Insurrections and others which have occurred or been attempted in the United States and elsewhere during the last two Centuries. With various Remarks. Collected from various Sources.* (New York, 1860.)

Columbia University *Studies in History, Economics and Public Law.* Edited by the faculty of political science. The useful volumes of this series for this field are:

W. L. Fleming's *Civil War and Reconstruction in Alabama,* 1905.

W. W. Davis's *The Civil War and Reconstruction in Florida,* 1913.

Clara Mildred Thompson's *Reconstruction in Georgia, Economic, Social, Political,* 1915.

J. G. de R. Hamilton's *Reconstruction in North Carolina,* 1914.

C. W. Ramsdell. *Reconstruction in Texas*, 1910.

Connecticut, Public Acts passed by the General Assembly of.

CROMWELL, J. W. *The Negro in American History: Men and Women Eminent in the Evolution of the American of African Descent.* (Washington, 1914.)

DAVIDSON, A., and STOWE, B. *A Complete History of Illinois from 1673 to 1873.* (Springfield, 1874.) It embraces the physical features of the country, its early explorations, aboriginal inhabitants, the French and British occupation, the conquest of Virginia, territorial condition and subsequent events.

DELANY, M. R. *The Condition, Elevation, Emigration and Destiny of the Colored People of the United States: politically considered.* (Philadelphia, 1852.)

DuBois, W. E. B. *The Philadelphia Negro: A Social Study. Together with a special report on domestic service by Isabel Eaton.* (Philadelphia, 1899.)

—— Atlanta University Publications, *The Negro Common School.* (Atlanta, 1901.)

—— *The Negro Church.* (Atlanta, 1903.)

—— and DILL, A. G. *The College-Bred Negro American.* (Atlanta, 1910.)

—— *The Negro American Artisan.* (Atlanta, 1912.)

DE TOQUEVILLE, ALEXIS CHARLES HENRI MAURICE CLEREL DE. *Democracy in America.* Translated by Henry Reeve. Four volumes. (London, 1835, 1840.)

EATON, JOHN. *Grant, Lincoln and the Freedmen: reminiscences of the Civil War with special reference to the work for the Contrabands, and the Freedmen of the Mississippi Valley.* (New York, 1907.)

EPSTEIN. *The Negro Migrant in Pittsburgh.* (Pittsburgh, 1917.)

Exposition of the Object and Plan of the American Union for the Relief and Improvement of the Colored Race. (Boston, 1835.)

FEE, JOHN G. *Anti-Slavery Manual.* (Maysville, 1848.)

FERTIG, JAMES WALTER. *The Secession and Reconstruction of Tennessee.* (Chicago, 1898.)

FROST, W. G. "*Appalachian America.*" (In vol. i of *The Americana.*) (New York, 1912.)

GARNETT, H. H. *The Past and Present Condition and the Destiny of the Colored Race.* (Troy, 1848.)

GREELY, HORACE. *The American Conflict.* A history of the great rebellion in the United States of America, 1860–64, its causes, incidents and results: intended to exhibit especially its moral and political phases, with the drift of progress of American opinion respecting human slavery from 1776 to the close of the war for its union. (Chicago, 1864.)

HAMMOND, M. B. *The Cotton Industry: an Essay in American Economic History.* It deals with the cotton cultuie and the cotton Trade. (New York, 1897.)

HART, A. B. *The Southern South.* (New York, 1906.)

HENSON, JOSIAH. *The Life of Josiah Henson.* (Boston, 1849.)

HERSHAW, L. M. *Peonage in the United States.* This is one of the American Negro Academy Papers. (Washington, 1912.)

HICKOK, CHARLES THOMAS. *The Negro in Ohio, 1802–1870.* (Cleveland, 1896.)

HODGKIN, THOMAS A. *Inquiry into the Merits of the American Colonization Society and Reply to the Charges brought against it with an Account of the British African Colonization Society.* (London, 1833.)

HOWE, SAMUEL G. *The Refugees from Slavery in Canada West. Report to the Freedmen's Inquiry Committee.* (Boston, 1864.)

HUTCHINS, THOMAS. *An Historical Narrative and Topographical Description of Louisiana and West Florida, comprehending the river Mississippi with its principal Branches and Settlements and the Rivers Pearl and Pescagoula.* (Philadelphia, 1784.)

Illinois, Laws of, passed by the General Assembly of.

Indiana, Laws passed by the State of.

JAY, JOHN. *The Correspondence and Public Papers of John Jay. First Chief Justice of the United States and President of the Continental Congress, Member of the Commission to negotiate the Treaty of Independence, Envoy to Great Britain, Governor of New York, etc., 1782–1793.* (New York and London, 1891.) Edited by Henry P.

Johnson, Professor of History in the College of the City of New York.

JAY, WILLIAM. *An Inquiry into the Character and Tendencies of the American Colonization and American Anti-Slavery Societies.* Second edition. (New York, 1835.)

JEFFERSON, THOMAS. *The Writings of Thomas Jefferson, Memorial Edition. Autobiography, Notes on Virginia, Parliamentary Mannual, Official Papers, Messages and Addresses, and other writings Official and Private, etc.* (Washington, 1903.)

Johns Hopkins University Studies in Historical and Political Science. H. B. Adams, Editor. (Baltimore, Johns Hopkins Press.) Among the useful volumes of this series are: J. R. Ficklen's *History of Reconstruction in Louisiana,* 1910. H. J. Eckenrode's *The Political History of Virginia during Reconstruction,* 1904.

LANGSTON, JOHN M. *From the Virginia Plantation to the National Capital; or, The First and Only Negro Representative in Congress from The Old Dominion.* (Hartford, 1894.)

LOCKE, M. S. *Anti-Slavery in America from the Introduction of African Slaves to the Prohibition of the Slave Trade, 1619–1808.* Radcliffe College Monographs, No. ii. (Boston, 1901.) A valuable work.

LYNCH, JOHN R. *The Facts of Reconstruction.* (New York, 1913.)

MADISON, JAMES. *Letters and Other Writings of James Madison Published by Order of Congress.* Four volumes. (Philadelphia, 1865.)

MAY, S. J. *Some Recollections of our Anti-Slavery Conflict.*

MONROE, JAMES. *The Writings of James Monroe, including a Collection of his public and private Papers and Correspondence now for the first time printed.* Edited by S. M. Hamilton. (Boston, 1900.)

MOORE, GEORGE H. *Notes on the History of Slavery in Massachusetts.* (New York, 1866.)

NEEDLES, EDWARD. *Ten Years' Progress or a Comparison of the State and Condition of the Colored People in the City of and County of Philadelphia from 1837 to 1847.* (Philadelphia, 1849.)

New Jersey, Acts of the General Assembly of.

Ohio, Laws of the General Assembly of.

OVINGTON, M. W.   *Half-a-Man.*   (New York, 1911.)   Treats of the Negro in the State of New York.   A few pages are devoted to the progress of the colored people.

PARRISH, JOHN.   *Remarks on the Slavery of the Black People; Addressed to the Citizens of the United States, particularly to those who are in legislative or executive Stations, particularly in the General or State Governments; and also to such Individuals as hold them in Bondage.*   (Philadelphia, 1806.)

PEARSON, E. W.   *Letters from Port Royal, written at the Time of the Civil War.*   (Boston, 1916.)

PEARSON, C. C.   *The Readjuster Movement in Virginia.*   (New Haven, 1917.)

Pennsylvania, Laws of the General Assembly of the State of.

PIERCE, E. L.   *The Freedmen of Port Royal, South Carolina, Official Reports.*   (New York, 1863.)

PIKE, JAMES S.   *The Prostrate State: South Carolina under Negro Government.*   (New York, 1874.)

PITTMAN, PHILIP.   *The Present State of European Settlements on the Mississippi with a geographic description of that river.*   (London, 1770.)

QUILLEN, FRANK U.   *The Color Line in Ohio.*   A History of Race Prejudice in a typical northern State.   (Ann Arbor, Mich., 1913.)

REYNOLDS, J. S.   *Reconstruction in South Carolina.*   (Columbia, 1905.)

Rhode Island, Acts and Resolves of.

RICE, DAVID.   *Slavery inconsistent with Justice and Good Policy: proved by a Speech delivered in the Convention held at Danville, Kentucky.*   (Philadelphia, 1792, and London, 1793.)

SCHERER, J. A. B.   *Cotton as a World Power.*   (New York, 1916.)   This is a study in the economic interpretation of History.   The contents of this book are a revision of a series of lectures at Oxford and Cambridge universities in the Spring of 1914 with the caption on Economic Causes in the American Civil War.

SIEBERT, WILBUR H.   *The Underground Railroad from Slavery to Freedom*, by W. H. Siebert, Associate Professor of History in the Ohio State University, with an Introduction by A. B. Hart. (New York, 1898.)

STARR, FREDERICK. *What shall be done with the people of color in the United States?* (Albany, 1862.) A discourse delivered in the First Presbyterian Church of Penn Yan, New York, November 2, 1862.

STILL, WILLIAM. *The Underground Railroad.* (Philadelphia, 1872.) This is a record of facts, authentic narratives, letters and the like, giving the hardships, hair-breadth escapes and death struggles of the slaves in their efforts for freedom as related by themselves and others or witnessed by the author.

The Jesuit Relations and Allied Documents, Travels and Explorations of the Jesuit Missionaries in New France, 1619–1791. The Original French, Latin, and Italian Texts with English Translations and Notes illustrated by Portraits, Maps, and Facsimiles. Edited by Reuben Gold Thwaites, Secretary of the State Historical Society of Wisconsin. (Cleveland, 1896.)

THOMPSON, GEORGE. *Speech at the Meeting for the Extension of Negro Apprenticeship.* (London, 1838.)

—— *The Free Church Alliance with Manstealers. Send back the Money. Great Anti-Slavery Meeting in the City Hall, Glasgow, containing the Speeches delivered by Messrs. Wright, Douglass, and Buffum from America, and by George Thompson of London, with a Summary Account of a Series of Meetings held in Edinburgh by the above named Gentlemen.* (Glasgow, 1846.)

TORREY, JESSE, JR. *A Portraiture of Domestic Slavery in the United States with Reflections on the Practicability of restoring the Moral Rights of the Slave, without impairing the legal Privileges of the Possessor, and a Project of a Colonial Asylum for Free Persons of Color, including Memoirs of Facts on the Interior Traffic in Slaves and on Kidnapping, Illustrated with Engravings by Jesse Torrey, Jr., Physician, Author of a Series of Essays on Morals and the Diffusion of Knowledge.* (Philadelphia, 1817.)

—— *American Internal Slave Trade; with Reflections on the project for forming a Colony of Blacks in Africa.* (London, 1822.)

TURNER, E. R. *The Negro in Pennsylvania.* (Washington, 1911.)

Tyrannical Libertymen: a Discourse upon Negro Slavery in the United States, composed at —— in New Hampshire: on the Late Federal Thanksgiving Day. (Hanover, N. H., 1795.)

WALKER, DAVID. *Walker's Appeal in Four Articles, together with a Preamble to the Colored Citizens of the World, but in particular and very expressly to those of the United States of America, Written in Boston, State of Massachusetts, September 28, 1829.* Second edition. (Boston, 1830.) Walker was a Negro who hoped to arouse his race to self-assertion.

WARD, CHARLES. *Contrabands.* (Salem, 1866.) This suggests an apprenticeship, under the auspices of the government, to build the Pacific Railroad.

WASHINGTON, B. T. *The Story of the Negro.* Two volumes. (New York, 1909.)

WASHINGTON, GEORGE. *The Writings of George Washington, being his Correspondence, Addresses, Messages, and other papers, official and private, selected and published from the original Manuscripts with the Life of the Author, Notes and Illustrations, by Jared Sparks.* (Boston, 1835.)

WEEKS, STEPHEN B. *Southern Quakers and Slavery. A Study in Institutional History.* (Baltimore, The Johns Hopkins Press, 1896.)

—— *The Anti-Slavery Sentiment in the South; with Unpublished Letters from John Stuart Mill and Mrs. Stowe.* (Southern History Association Publications, Volume ii, No. 2, Washington, D. C., April, 1898.)

WILLIAMS, G. W. *A History of the Negro Troops in the War of the Rebellion, 1861–1865, preceded by a Review of the military Services of Negroes in ancient and modern Times.* (New York, 1888.)

—— *History of the Negro Race in the United States from 1619–1880. Negroes as Slaves, as Soldiers, and as Citizens: together with a preliminary Consideration of the Unity of the Human Family, an historical Sketch of Africa and an Account of the Negro Governments of Sierra Leone and Liberia.* (New York, 1883.)

WOODSON, C. G. *The Education of the Negro Prior to 1861.* (New York and London, 1915.) This is a history of the Education of the Colored People of the United States from the beginning of slavery to the Civil War.

WOOLMAN, JOHN. *The Works of John Woolman. In two Parts, Part I: A Journal of the Life, Gospel-Labors, and Christian Experiences of that faithful Minister of Christ, John Woolman, late of Mount Holly in the Province of New Jersey.* (London, 1775.)

—— *Same, Part Second. Containing his last Epistle and other Writings.* (London, 1775.)

—— *Some Considerations on the Keeping of Negroes. Recommended to the Professors of Christianity of every Denomination.* (Philadelphia, 1754.)

—— *Considerations on Keeping Negroes; Recommended to the Professors of Christianity of every Denomination. Part the Second.* (Philadelphia, 1762.)

WRIGHT, R. R., JR. *The Negro in Pennsylvania.* (Philadelphia, 1912.)

MAGAZINES

The African Methodist Episcopal Church Review. The following articles:

The Negro as an Inventor. By R. R. Wright, vol. ii, p. 397.

Negro Poets, vol. iv, p. 236.

The Negro in Journalism, vols. vi, p. 309, and xx, p. 137. p. 137.

The African Repository; Published by the American Colonization Society from 1826 to 1832. A very good source for Negro history both in this country and Liberia. Some of its most valuable articles are:

Learn Trades or Starve, by Frederick Douglass, vol. xxix, p. 137. Taken from Frederick Douglass's Paper.

Education of the Colored People, by a highly respectable gentleman of the South, vol. xxx, pp. 194, 195 and 196.

Elevation of the Colored Race, a memorial circulated in North Carolina, vol. xxxi, pp. 117 and 118.

A lawyer for Liberia, a sketch of Garrison Draper, vol. xxxiv, pp. 26 and 27.

The American Economic Review.
The American Journal of Social Science.
The American Journal of Political Economy.
The American Law Review.
The American Journal of Sociology.
The Atlantic Monthly.
The Colonizationist and Journal of Freedom. The author has been able to find only the volume which contains the numbers for the year 1834.
The Christian Examiner.
The Cosmopolitan.
The Crisis. A record of the darker races published by the National Association for the Advancement of Colored People.
Dublin Review.
The Forum.
The Independent.
The Journal of Negro History.
The Maryland Journal of Colonization. Published as the official organ of the Maryland Colonization Society. Among its important articles are: *The Capacities of the Negro Race,* vol. iii, p. 367; and *The Educational Facilities of Liberia,* vol. vii, p. 223.
The Nation.
The Non-Slaveholder. Two volumes of this publication are now found in the Library of Congress.
The Outlook.
Public Opinion.
The Southern Workman. Volume xxxvii contains Dr. R. R. Wright's valuable dissertation on *Negro Rural Communities in India.*
The Spectator.
The Survey.
The World's Work.

NEWSPAPERS

District of Columbia.
  The Daily National Intelligencer.
Louisiana.
  The New Orleans Commercial Bulletin.
  The New Orleans Times-Picayune.

Maryland.
   The Maryland Journal and Baltimore Advertiser.
   The Maryland Gazette.
   Dunlop's Maryland Gazette or The Baltimore Advertiser.
Massachusetts.
   The Liberator.
Mississippi.
   The Vicksburg Daily Commercial.
New York.
   The New York Daily Advertiser.
   The New York Tribune.
   The New York Times.

INDEX

Adams, Henry, leader of the exodus to Kansas, 135
Akron, friends of fugitives in, 30
Alton Telegraph, comment of, 113
Anderson, promoter of settling of Negroes in Jamaica, 79
Anti-slavery, leaders of the movement, became more helpful to the refugees, 34, 35
Anti-slavery sentiment, of two kinds, 3
American Federation of Labor, attitude of, toward Negro labor, 191
Appalachian highland, settlers of, aided fugitives, 31–34; exodus of Negroes to, 146
Arkansas, drain of laborers to, 120

Ball, J. P., a contractor, 95
Ball, Thomas, a contractor, 95
Barclay, interest of, in the sending of Negroes to Jamaica, 79
Barrett, Owen A., discoverer of a remedy, 90
Bates, owner of slaves at St. Genevieve, 7
Beauvais, owner of slaves, Upper Louisiana, 7
Benezet, Anthony, plan of, to colonize Negroes in West, 9; interest of, in settling Negroes in the West, 61
Berlin Cross Roads, Negroes of, 24
Bibb, Henry, interest of, in colonization, 79

Birney, James G., promoter of the migration of the Negroes, 35; press of, destroyed by mob in Cincinnati, 57
Black Friday, riot of, in Portsmouth, 57
Blackburn, Thornton, a fugitive claimed in Detroit, 59–60
Boll weevil, a cause of migration, 169
Boston, friends of fugitives in, 31
Boyce, Stanbury, went with his father to Trinidad in the fifties, 78
Boyd, Henry, a successful mechanic in Cincinnati, 95
Brannagan, Thomas, advocate of colonizing the Negroes in the West, 10; interest of, in settling Negroes in the West, 61
Brissot de Warville, observations of, on Negroes in the West, 12
British Guiana, attractive to free Negroes, 68
Brooklyn, Illinois, a Negro community, 30
Brown, John, in the Appalachian highland, 33–34
Brown County, Ohio, Negroes in, 25
Buffalo, friends of fugitives in, 30
Butler, General. holds Negroes as contraband, 107; policy of, followed by General Wood and General Banks, 102

212

270219-300-1-60W